Our Greatest Journalists

Fifty Years of the Oklahoma Journalism Hall of Fame

Lead Editor: Joe Hight

Series Editor: Gini Moore Campbell
Contributing Editors: Ralph Schaefer, Lindel Hutson, & Billie Rodely
Student Editor: Emily Siddiqui

ISBN: 978-1-938923-50-0
Library of Congress Control Number: 2020902315

Book and Cover Design by photogDESIGN.com

Printed in Canada

OKLAHOMA HALL *of* FAME
PUBLISHING

1400 Classen Drive
Oklahoma City, Oklahoma 73106
405.235.4458
www.OklahomaHoF.com

DEDICATION

This book is dedicated to Oklahoma Journalism Hall of Fame founders Dr. Ray Tassin and Dennie Hall, to those who have been inducted in or served the Oklahoma Journalism Hall of Fame and journalism in Oklahoma, and to those who have bravely fought to maintain our country's First Amendment freedoms. Without you, the Oklahoma Journalism Hall of Fame and this book would not be possible.

TABLE OF CONTENTS

INTRODUCTION
the pioneering spirit
By Joe Hight, 2013 Inductee

The Watergate scandal that would lead to United States President Richard Nixon's resignation was at its dawn when the Oklahoma Journalism Hall of Fame began at Central State University.

Watergate would spawn and inspire a new generation of journalists, some of whom would be inducted many years later. But, at the time of that first induction in 1971, the Hall of Fame reflected a pioneering spirit. And a sense of humor.

"Now folks, all I know is what little news I read every day in the papers," coined Will Rogers, humorist, columnist, author, radio personality, and movie star, in a radio program in 1923. It was later edited to "All I know is what I read in the papers."

Rogers is among the nearly 470 journalists inducted into the Hall of Fame. Inductees represent more than 100 years of journalism history. There are journalists who covered wars abroad and battles within the Oklahoma State Capitol. Journalists involved in bitter newspaper rivalries. Those who opened newspapers, radio stations, and television stations, representing the smallest news organizations and the largest ones. They

taught and provided mentoring not only to each other, but to generations of future journalists. They wrote books, many books. They fought for civil rights and for our First Amendment freedoms. They rarely backed down in fulfilling their watchdog roles or providing commentary about it.

The story of Oklahoma, the nation, and the world has been chronicled through the decades by men and women of diverse backgrounds and interests whose devotion to spreading the word has been recognized by the Hall of Fame.

You will see all 468 journalists and the six Lifetime Achievement Award recipients featured in this book. However, when I conceived the idea for this book, I wanted it to be more personal. I wanted the men and women in the Hall of Fame to tell the stories. That's why this book is devoted primarily to personal essays or vignettes by Hall of Fame members about others they admired or about themselves. You will also see stories told about certain inductees we were not able to meet.

In all, 28 different writers contributed to this book. Countless others contributed photographs. Most were Hall of Fame members themselves, connected closely to a Hall of Fame member or wanted to learn more about a member. Each had a personal connection to the story they told.

You will read not only about the history of the Oklahoma Journalism Hall of Fame, but also how its members helped shape Oklahoma history.

Hall of Fame members had many defining moments in their careers, from the assassination of John F. Kennedy and Watergate to the Penn Square Bank collapse and prison riots. The bombing of the Alfred P. Murrah Federal Building in downtown Oklahoma City is depicted in a special section of this book.

Most of all, you will read about how all Hall of Fame members embodied the pioneering spirit in their own lives. Enough of the spirit to be chosen for Oklahoma's highest journalistic honor and for a Hall of Fame that will forever remember their legacies.

Several staff members of the *Oklahoma City Times,* in 1909, when it was still a competing paper. The *Times* was purchased by The Oklahoma Publishing Company six years later. Courtesy of the Oklahoma Publishing Company, Cuff Stuff Magazine, March-April 1973.

THE HISTORY
the land run to launch a hall of fame
By Joe Hight, 2013 Inductee

Dennie Hall was only 34 years old in June 1969 when he arrived as a new faculty member at Central State College. Dr. Ray Tassin, the journalism department chairman, knew Hall was a historian. Almost immediately, he approached him with an idea.

"Tassin said he wanted to start a hall of fame," Hall said.

But what Hall revealed to me in the living room of his Edmond home more than 50 years later showed Tassin's competitiveness, especially when it came to a larger university 35 miles to the south. The 85-year-old Hall talked about the Hall of Fame while his television blared news in the background and as his 13-year-old cat Tabitha pawed me for attention.

"He wanted to get one underway before OU did. There were rumors that OU wanted one," he said. "He wanted to beat OU."

So, the land run for the first journalism hall of fame began. Central State "pushed a little faster," Hall said, and launched the Hall of Fame ahead of the Sooners.

While Tassin assumed the role of director that first year, Hall did the behind-the-scenes work in organizing not only the first inductions in 1971, but subsequent classes as well. The Hall of Fame started simply, its roots imbedded with the Oklahoma Press Association (OPA) and the college's chapter of The Society of Professional Journalists, Sigma Delta Chi. Tassin handed out the certificates from the first class at an OPA event.

Those simple beginnings launched what has become a "who's who" of journalism in Oklahoma and the country. The first class was a testament to that: Will Rogers, Roscoe Dunjee, Jim Lucas, Edward King Gaylord, Stanley Vestal, Richard Lloyd Jones, Sr., H.H. Herbert, Milt Reynolds, and Bill Martineau.

"No women were included at the beginning," Hall wrote during the Hall of Fame's 45th anniversary, "but that would slowly change."

The first woman inducted into the Hall of Fame was writer Alice Lee Marriott in 1973. The Hall of Fame continued to evolve, as did the university from Central State College to Central State University to the University of Central Oklahoma (UCO). The annual Hall of Fame event went from a meeting or dinner in conjunction with the OPA to an annual luncheon at UCO with more than 300 attendees for the 49th class. The exception will be the 50th year celebration during an evening banquet at the Oklahoma History Center. The luncheon format at UCO will return with the 51st class.

The OPA has been involved with the Hall of Fame since its inception. Hall said nine inductees were selected the first year, because that was the number that could fit, with photos, on the Hall of Fame certificate. Tassin made sure they were framed and placed on a display wall, originally in the Communications Building. The certificates with the nine inductee biographies and photos are still given out, and they are still framed and placed on a wall. However, today, Hall of Fame inductees also are given plaques featuring their photo and year of induction along with lapel pins signifying they are members of the Oklahoma Journalism Hall of Fame.

The first selection committee was comprised of two members—Tassin and Hall. Hall remembers the committee grew to three or four members. Today the committee is made up of ten members and includes a representative from the Association of Oklahoma Broadcasters. One of Hall's goals was to increase the diversity of the inductees, including broadcasters.

After years, Tassin relinquished the role so Hall could become the director. Hall held the position for 15 years, until the 25th anniversary of the Hall of Fame. Hall spent many of those years teaching and as adviser of the student newspaper, *The Vista*, where I first met him in 1976. I became its editor in 1979. Dr. Terry Clark then became the Hall of Fame director and held the position for 21 years.

I took the position in 2016 and promised Hall I wouldn't hold the position for as long as he or Clark.

"Well, we were a lot younger than you were, too," said Hall, with his dry sense of humor.

As director, "Mr. Hall," as I continue to call him, did extensive research and found names that were not included in the Hall of Fame class. As a result, Frank Hilton Greer and Leslie Niblack were both inducted in 1982. Hall designed the first letterhead and brochure, and started seeing the Hall of Fame "growing in prestige and circumstance."

That growth continued under Clark, who assumed the role as department chair and then continued after he stepped down as chair after 19 years in 2009. Under his leadership, the Hall of Fame relocated from the Communications Building to the Nigh University Center, just down the hallway from where the annual luncheon is held. It was moved on the Hall of Fame's 40th anniversary. That area now displays the biographies and photos of members, including the first posthumous class that was inducted in 2005. Clark also secured an annual budget for the Hall of Fame and started creating special publications for the 40th and 45th anniversaries. He also started giving scholarships, one in ethics endowed by the family of journalist Brian J. Walke and another in honor of the Oklahoma Press Association, which provides funding in the form of a monthly donation given in the name of Hall of Fame members who judge its monthly contests.

"Working with the Oklahoma Journalism Hall of Fame is an honor and dream job as a journalist, weekly newspaperman and grateful member of the Hall of Fame," Clark wrote. Even after retirement, Clark remains a part-time consultant.

As I talked to Mr. Hall about the past, I started thinking about my short time as director, how the Hall of Fame has changed over time, and its future. It now has video introductions of the nine Hall of Fame inductees produced in the Mass Communication Department instead of speeches that sometimes stretched to 30 minutes or longer. The membership lapel

Dr. Reba Collins looks over publications with Dr. Ray Tassin, Henry Hunt, and Dr. Stan Hoig. They were all faculty at Central State College during the 1960s.

Terry Clark, retired Oklahoma Journalism Hall of Fame Director, served as UCO Journalism Department Chairman. He owned the *Waurika News-Democrat* and worked at the *Duncan Banner*. Here, he accepts the Milt Phillips Award from the Oklahoma Press Association.

pins have been added. The Nigh University Center office is being turned into a small Hall of Fame museum, and we are celebrating the 50th anniversary. The Oklahoma Journalism Hall of Fame also will have its own website and its first documentary.

Without the competitiveness of Tassin, the steadfast organization and historical knowledge of Hall, and the development and expansion capabilities of Clark, the Hall of Fame perhaps would be nonexistent, as it is in other states.

From that simple and competitive beginning, the Oklahoma Journalism Hall of Fame has grown to become the state's most prestigious journalistic honor and among the highest honors an individual can receive. It's a place where Oklahoma's greatest journalists reside forever.

"I have many memories of the Hall of Fame," Hall said, reminding me that I needed to focus on him, the only person still living with knowledge of its inception. "I am pleased that we have brought it to the 50-year mark. I'm pleased that it's gone from a simple format to a much more elaborate organization and ceremony."

College newsrooms are often the launchpads of many journalists' careers—and long-term relationships. Dennie Hall, past Oklahoma Journalism Hall of Fame Director and member since 1999, works at the top of the copy desk rim with student staff members, from left, Doug Folks, Joe Hight, Dwayne Long, and Terri Dobson in *The Vista's* office at Central State University, later, the University of Central Oklahoma. Hall was the adviser to the student newspaper at the time the photo was taken in the late 1970s. Doug and Terri later married and are celebrating their 39th anniversary in 2020. Hight, who has been a Hall of Fame member since 2013, credits Hall as being not only his mentor but his inspiration to become a journalist.

THE 1970s
the opening years of journalistic history

The names that shaped Oklahoma and American journalistic history were among the 79 journalists inducted into the Oklahoma Journalism Hall of Fame during its opening decade.

After the Hall of Fame was founded by Dr. Ray Tassin and Dennie Hall in 1970, the first class was inducted in 1971. One of the first nine inductees was Milton W. Reynolds, whose 20-year crusade was credited in opening Oklahoma to settlement. Another was famed humorist and columnist Will Rogers. War correspondent Jim Lucas was the first Pulitzer Prize winner inducted into the Hall that same year. They were joined by Roscoe Dunjee, the son of a slave who founded *The Black Dispatch*, the first African-American newspaper in Oklahoma.

"With courageous editorials he crusaded for civil rights before it was fashionable—or even safe—to do so," Dunjee's Hall of Fame biography read. "He also founded various civil rights groups, earning a reputation as the father of the Black civil rights struggle in Oklahoma."

Others inducted during the decade include news pioneers such as Edward King Gaylord, Ben Blackstock, Eugene Pulliam, Paul Harvey, Paul Miller, and Ernie Schultz.

The first woman inducted into the Hall of Fame was author Alice Lee Marriott in 1973. She was followed in 1977 by Wauhillau Lahay, the first Oklahoman to serve as Washington Press Club president.

The first couple inducted together into the hall was O.H. and Hattie Mae Lachenmeyer in 1976. The Lachenmeyers edited and published seven community newspapers in Oklahoma.

Vance H. Trimble, an author and Pulitzer Prize winner, was inducted in 1974. In 2020 he continued to live in Wewoka at 106 years old. Trimble remembered years later that each member received a simple "Certificate of Award" noting being "selected to the Oklahoma Journalism Hall of Fame for outstanding service to the journalism profession."

Despite the simplicity of its beginnings, those inducted in the 1970s were names that would live on as some of the country's greatest journalists, a standard that would continue into the following decades.

Lying in state at an eastside funeral home is a dummy representing segregation in Oklahoma City. The photo appeared in the August 27, 1963 of the *Oklahoma Times*. Jim Lucas photo. Courtesy of the Oklahoma Historical Society.

WILL ROGERS
he roped in a generation and beyond
By Joseph H. Carter, Sr., 1992 Inductee

Will Rogers was born in 1879 on a sprawling Cherokee ranch near Oologah, Indian Territory. After working cattle and riding the range, Will Rogers circumnavigated the globe three times. He launched his show business career as a roper in Texas Jack's Wild West Show in Lady Smith, South Africa, and wrote 3,483 columns syndicated by *The New York Times* for hundreds of newspapers. Additionally, he authored six best-selling, humor-filled books and uncounted magazine yarns.

With down-home language, off-beat style, crude spelling and quotable one-liners, Will Rogers' writing easily earned him a slot in the 1971 inaugural class of the Oklahoma Journalism Hall of Fame, more than three decades after his death.

Atop journalism feats, Will Rogers starred in 71 movies that often topped world box offices. He was an actor and comedian on Broadway, including a long stint in the famous "Ziegfeld Follies" after playing in vaudeville and wild west shows. He was also a pioneer radio commentator.

While show business was a main contributor to his undocumented total wealth that doubtlessly would have capped multi-millions in contemporary dollars, $2,500 fees for a magazine feature were not uncommon for his "must-read," funny political punditry.

Will Rogers' bronze statue looms in the National Statuary Hall Collection in the United States Capitol. He is "keeping an eye on Congress," a quote he invented and a trait of his deep purposes.

On a personal level, while he nominally wore a business suit when performing, Will Rogers' self-portrait was that of a cowboy. His array of trick roping skills has never been fully duplicated. An extant 1922 two-reel movie titled "The Ropin' Fool" co-stars him, horses and his lariat.

Despite world fame, home always was Oklahoma for Will Rogers, who was officially dubbed William Penn Adair Rogers when born in a log-walled cabin. His life is a drama reported in scores of biographies, a feature film and in the 1991 musical *The Will Rogers Follies: A Life in Review* that played 982 times on Broadway.

The Papers of Will Rogers, published by the University of Oklahoma Press, required 3,002 pages in five volumes and is prized in most academic libraries worldwide.

Beyond 2,817 terse daily and 666 expansive weekly syndicated columns published in as many as 600 newspapers, Will Rogers was a staple feature writer for the *Saturday Evening Post*. In 19 volumes, these writings were published again by Oklahoma State University from 1973 to 1983.

In 1928, Will Rogers penned a series of satire feature yarns in *Life* Magazine, hyping himself as a prank candidate seeking nomination for president. It launched a genre of comedians who borrowed the theme.

Will Rogers was in a single-engine seaplane with the legendary one-eyed pilot Wiley Post on August 15, 1935. They flew around Alaska and were headed toward Point Barrow when they saw an Eskimo encampment and landed. With directions pointing northward, they were about 200 feet aloft when the craft nose-dived into shallow water. The two Oklahomans died on impact, capturing banner headlines in papers worldwide. Post is interred in Oklahoma City's Memorial Park Cemetery. Will Rogers' tomb is at the Will Rogers Memorial Museum, a nine-gallery museum in Claremore, just nine miles from the Dog Iron Ranch of his birth.

Joseph H. Carter, Sr. not only wrote about Will Rogers, but he also performed as Will Rogers throughout his life, including 180 shows in Branson, Missouri.

JOSEPH H. CARTER, SR., DR. REBA COLLINS, & BOB G. BURKE
hall of famers who have kept Will Rogers' legacy alive
By Joseph H. Carter, Sr., 1992 Inductee

Will Rogers' success and fame as a self-taught journalist won him a membership in the Oklahoma Journalism Hall of Fame. Three other Hall of Fame members have worked to keep alive Rogers' legacy.

Dr. Reba Collins and Joseph H. Carter, Sr. were directors of the Will Rogers Memorial Commission. They also churned out books and publications based on their long studies of Will Rogers' life from 1879-1935.

The third Hall of Fame member, Bob G. Burke, wrote a definitive book on Wiley Post, the Oklahoma aviator who was piloting the single-engine plane that crashed near Point Barrow, Alaska, killing both Will Rogers and Post.

Burke also edited *Will Rogers: American Wordsmith* written by Collins and published in 2011 with a foreword by Governor George Nigh.

Joseph H. Carter, Sr. 2019, UCO Photographic Services.

Joseph H. Carter, Sr. as Will Rogers, 2019, UCO Photographic Services.

While a top aide to Governor David Hall, Carter recognized that Dr. Collins had written her doctoral dissertation on Will Rogers. He then championed and handled her appointment to the Memorial Commission where she later was tapped as director.

During her years directing the Claremore museum, Collins edited several books refreshing the works, history and legacy of Will Rogers, who wrote more than 4,000 syndicated newspaper pundit columns and a half-dozen books.

Born in the Cherokee Nation near present-day Oologah, Will Rogers also starred in 71 movies, played in wild west shows, vaudeville, and was a famous Broadway comedian. He is known as "Oklahoma's Favorite Son."

Carter and his wife, Michelle, were both Memorial Commission directors who raised financing and oversaw publication of the five-volume, 3,002-page *The Papers of Will Rogers*, published by University of Oklahoma Press.

Joseph H. Carter, Sr. and his wife, Michelle, served as directors of the Will Rogers Memorial Commission in Claremore, Oklahoma for 20 years. 2019, UCO Photographic Services.

Carter, a newspaperman and wire service correspondent for 17 years, wrote two biographies of Will Rogers published by Harper-Collins and Gibbs Smith Publishers. Carter also wrote specialty yarns about Will Rogers that were published in several magazines.

ALICE LEE MARRIOTT
the many firsts of a Hall of Famer
By Emily Siddiqui, Student Editor

As a writer, anthropologist, scholar, and historian, Alice Lee Marriott did much to deserve her title as the first woman inducted into the Oklahoma Journalism Hall of Fame in 1973.

She was born in Wilmette, Illinois in 1910. Her family moved to Oklahoma City in 1917, where many of her passions took root. Marriott's love for people and words began at a young age. She started reading when she was just two years old and later wrote plays for her siblings to act out. At Oklahoma City's Central High School, she was awarded her first literary prize for one of her stories.

After malaria compromised her health, Marriott quit her job at the Muskogee Public Library to enroll at the University of Oklahoma to learn more about American Indians. There, she became the first woman to earn a bachelor's degree in anthropology. She worked on several historical sites, including the Spiro Mounds in Oklahoma.

As a specialist in ethnology—the study of living cultures—she wrote at least 20 books and dozens of major articles on history, folklore, biography, and personal reminiscences. She wrote for young adults and children alike. Scholars rank her writing among the best of its kind, particularly the work on the cultures of American Indians.

After World War II, she lived in Nambe, New Mexico, where she worked on *Maria, The Potter of San Ildefonso*, her most famous book. Other works include *The Ten Grandmothers*, the story of the Kiowa, *Greener Fields*, and *Hell on Horses and Women*. She and Carol K. Rachlin

Ernie Schultz was looking for a weekend news anchor and weekday reporter/photographer. I applied and got the job, which was the start of decades of association with and admiration for Ernie Schultz.

Channel 4 was a visual news factory, including an orientation film showing screen direction and how to shoot reversal questions, principles of the way Hollywood used to film movies. We were efficient, ready for the next day's events but completely flexible. The Oklahoma State Capitol, City Hall, conventions, and regular beats were all covered. We went "live" from some locations with a converted bus.

WKY-TV News covered the hearings during the Supreme Court scandal of the 1960s. The quality and dependability of WKY-TV news was so good it was almost considered another NBC News Bureau. And Ernie Schultz was responsible for that.

We strove to ensure we got it right. Schultz remembered an anchor who used the term "suicide," but authorities later determined it was an "accidental" death.

"Died by his own hand would have been safer," Schultz said.

Schultz loved offbeat features like the horse that somehow climbed up into the hayloft of an Oklahoma City barn and had to be hauled down.

One time, Schultz used French to lighten up newsroom banter about an unsavory politician by blurting out "hors de combat by now."

The Scout motto "Be Prepared" fit in the newsroom.

Schultz loved to fly and kept a plane at Expressway Airpark near WKY-TV. I walked in one morning and was told we were flying 200 miles to photograph an area affected by Oklahoma's brutal drought. Exposed film was placed between two small pillows stuck together with gaffers tape for a soft landing. I said "OK."

He flew low on the east side of the old WKY-TV building where several employees were waiting. I said, "bombs away." Didn't even need a Norden bombsight!

Video seamlessly replaced film at Channel 4. The results helped draw outstanding photographers who adapted to video, like the late national award-winning news photographer Darrell Barton, whose work has been aired on *60 Minutes* and *48 Hours*, and the journalist Bob Dotson whose "The American Story" aired on NBC's *Today* for decades.

Before leaving to become the first elected president of the Radio Television News Directors Association (RTNDA), now the Radio Television News Association and later press secretary for U.S. Senator Don Nickles, Schultz played an important role in at least

Ernie Schultz, a pioneer television newsman at Oklahoma City's WKY-TV, had a no-nonsense approach in telling people about events in the state. A private pilot, he would fly photographers to news events in Oklahoma, then get the film back in time for a newscast.

Ernie Schultz and George Tomek go over the assignments for the day.

From left, Ernie Schultz, George Tomek, Len Sassenrath, and Lon Becker work in the newsroom in the '60s.

two journalistic changes for Oklahoma.

He promoted Pam Henry to become the first female news anchor in Oklahoma and was instrumental in the movement to allow cameras in the courtroom. Decades later, television viewers could see testimony in the 2019 federal trial involving opioid manufacturers and the heartache the painkillers caused.

Schultz was inducted into the Oklahoma Journalism Hall of Fame in 1978. He left us in November 2017 at 87 years old. His legacy will last forever.

THE LEGENDS OF BROADCASTING
many started in Oklahoma radio, now many in Hall of Fame
By Jerry Bohnen, 2006 Inductee

Oklahoma's long list of "radio" journalists are among some of the nation's most widely heard reporters, becoming legends in America's broadcasting industry. They were known for their coverage of wars, space launches, and for their leadership in radio newsrooms. Others were known for their place in history as the nation's taste for news led to the development of television and the creation of "anchormen."

Paul Harvey. Frank McGee. Douglas Edwards. Jim Hartz. Mike Boettcher. These Oklahoma Journalism Hall of Fame members are among the dozens of nationally known journalists such as Walter Cronkite and Curt Gowdy who either got their start in radio or ventured there from newspaper jobs.

For some, they entered the world of radio news when radio was still growing up, and they were part of the great experiment to put sound to the news of the day. They were among the first to experiment with "live" remote coverage of football games, parades, and other events. Theirs was news coverage often through telephone lines or from remote transmitter trucks.

Walter Cronkite might be among the best-known. He got his start

doing live sports coverage of University of Oklahoma (OU) football games. It was 1937 when he went to work for WKY Radio in Oklahoma City. Some 25 years later, he took over the *CBS Evening News with Walter Cronkite.*

The man he replaced was Ada, Oklahoma, native Douglas Edwards. While Edwards never worked in radio in Oklahoma, he got his start as a 15-year-old boy in Troy, Alabama, and eventually landed with CBS Radio in 1942. From there, he became the first major anchor for CBS Television before being replaced by Cronkite in 1962.

Curt Gowdy broadcast major sports events for ABC and NBC sports. He got his start at a small station in Cheyenne, Wyoming, before landing a job at KOMA Radio in 1946, where he was hired to cover OU football.

Frank McGee, who attended high school in Seminole and Norman, started his broadcast career with KGFF Radio in Shawnee in 1940 before moving to television and eventually becoming "one of television's most prominent newsmen" in the 1960s.

Another NBC correspondent, James "Jim" Hartz, got his start with KOME and KRMG radio stations in Tulsa where he did newscasts. His radio work led to KOTV in Tulsa, then to NBC where he co-anchored the *Today Show* with Barbara Walters and won five Emmy awards.

Mike Boettcher first tasted broadcast journalism working for WBBZ Radio in his hometown of Ponca City, Oklahoma, and for KEBC and KTOK radio stations in Oklahoma City. He later worked as a foreign correspondent for CNN, ABC, and the BBC.

Others who made radio their medium of choice came from newspapers and stayed on the broadcast side of journalism, winning prestigious honors such as the Edward R. Murrow Award. Some toiled in smaller markets, filling the airwaves with the news that included obituaries, birth announcements, city council meetings, and, of course, the police blotter.

Billie Rodely became known for being among the first female

news director, he was credited with building the station's news and weather reputation.

- A 2012 inductee, Neal Kennedy was born in a military hospital on Oahu in Hawaii. After his dad's military career, the family settled in Norman. Kennedy worked at the University of Central Oklahoma campus station in Edmond before joining WKY Radio. He then headed up the turnpike to spend 24 years as a reporter and assistant news director at KVOO in Tulsa, before finishing out his career crosstown at KRMG.

- Lis Exon is a graduate of The University of Tulsa and a 2017 inductee. She reported for campus station KWGS, as well as commercial radio stations KXXO and KELI in Tulsa. She jumped to television at Channel 2 in Tulsa. She would later report for TV stations in Denver, Colorado, in Orlando, Florida, and in Houston, Texas. Exon would return to Channel 2 and finish her career at the Oklahoma Educational Television Authority.

Finally, I would join Exon as a Hall of Fame member in 2017, but took the opposite path, opting to end my career at The University of Tulsa radio station KWGS. A product of OSU, I worked at KTOK in Oklahoma City before becoming news director at KAKC, in my native Tulsa. I also was the operation manager for a chain of stations headquartered in Joplin during the 1980s. I returned to Tulsa to spend 20 years at KRMG, 18 as news director.

Now you know the rest of the story about how Oklahoma Journalism Hall of Famers made an impact not only on Tulsa radio but on the nation's airwaves, too.

THE FAMILIES
Dyers lead with six Hall of Fame members
By Ray Dyer & Andy Rieger, 2010 Inductees

Oklahoma newspaper pioneers simultaneously built their hometowns while collectively lifting their young state.

Families were and are the cornerstone of the state's weekly and daily publications. They had well-known Oklahoma names, such as Gaylord, Lorton, Jones, Livermore, Mayo, Dyer, Reid, Muchmore, Hruby, Phillips, Pate, Nance, McBride, Engleman, Langdon, Gourley, Hefton, Perry, Stamper, Schnoebelen, Cain, Wade, Walter, Ferguson, Choate, Curtin, Fields, Shepler, Bentley, Lansden, Bellatti, Goodwin, and dozens of others.

Many are in the Oklahoma Journalism Hall of Fame.

The Dyer family tops all of them with six members, followed closely by other families with four members or honorees, including the Gaylords, Fergusons, and Goodwins.

Some family newspapers were started by moves to Oklahoma's largest cities.

Edward King Gaylord stepped off the train in Oklahoma City in 1902 with the intention of investing in a local newspaper. A Chicago publisher had recommended he check out the post-Land Run boomtown that Oklahoma City was becoming. He liked what he saw and bought into *The Oklahoman* for $5,000, thus beginning a family newspaper dynasty that spanned three generations.

Eugene Lorton moved to Tulsa from Walla Walla, Washington, and bought an interest in the *Tulsa World*. He was the newspaper's editor in 1911 and became sole owner and publisher in 1917. Around that time Richard Lloyd Jones, Sr. bought the *Tulsa Democrat* and renamed it the *Tulsa Tribune*, an afternoon newspaper that ceased operations in 1992 when the *World* bought its remaining assets. The *Tulsa World* would remain in the Lorton family until 2013.

Others were bound to smaller communities.

As a young man during the Great Depression, Ed Livermore, Sr. was sweeping out the front office of the *Hobart Democrat-Chief* one evening when two men approached him to see the publisher Everett Pate. The men were there to offer Pate $65,000 to sell his newspaper. "That was a day I'll never forget," Livermore recalled. "That's what got me in the newspaper business." He and his wife, Melba, met at the University of Oklahoma (OU) and eventually owned newspapers throughout the state, including in Claremore, Sapulpa, Edmond, Guthrie, Catoosa, Midwest City, Del City, Oklahoma City, and Mineral Wells, Texas. His son, Ed Livermore, Jr., was publisher of the *Edmond Sun* until it was sold in 1999.

Others like the Dyers have stood out as being among the families who have remained in Oklahoma. The Dyers are among those who have remained committed to one community—El Reno.

Ray J. Dyer came to Oklahoma from Kansas. He purchased the *El Reno Tribune* in 1934 from Eugene Pulliam. The *Tribune* has remained in the Dyer family, operated by the Dyer brothers, Sean and Ray, and their sister, Erin Dyer Thompson. Sisters Shanon Eaton and Tricia Hobson have also worked at the newspaper, along with other family members.

Ray J. Dyer was inducted into the Hall of Fame in 1979. He was followed by his son John R. "Jack" Dyer, who was inducted in 1982, one year after his death. In 1992, the elder Dyer's daughter, Mary Kay Dyer, was inducted into the Hall of Fame. In 2010, Jack's sons, Ray Dyer and Sean Dyer, were inducted, while in 2014 his daughter, Kelly Dyer Fry, was added to the Hall of Fame.

The Dyers have been reporters, editors, publishers, and presidents of various organizations, including four as president of the Oklahoma Press Association Board of Directors.

They all take pride in their family newspaper.

Over the years, many Dyer family members have worked at the *El Reno Tribune*. From helping to run the press to taking photos, writing stories, keeping the books, and selling advertising, it's been a family operation. Many employees without the Dyer name have spent more than 20, 30, or even 40 years as part of the *Tribune* family.

"They're all hall of famers in our books," Sean Dyer said.

MEMBERS INDUCTED IN THE 1970s

— 1971

Walter S. Campbell, pen name Stanley Vestal (1887-1957), first Rhodes Scholar from the state, author of 24 books, professor of literature and writing at the University of Central Oklahoma, developed the Professional Writing Program at the University of Oklahoma.

Roscoe Dunjee (1883-1965), founder, editor, and publisher of *The Black Dispatch*, the first black newspaper in the state, founder of various civil rights groups, earned a reputation as the father of the black civil rights struggle in Oklahoma.

Edward King Gaylord (1873-1974), owner of the Oklahoma Publishing Company, adding the *Oklahoma City Times*, *Oklahoma Farmer-Stockman*, WKY-TV, and other enterprises; pioneer of newspaper innovations, including the use of computers in composition.

H.H. Herbert (1888-1980), founder and director of the H.H. Herbert School of Journalism at the University of Oklahoma (1913), founder of the Oklahoma Intercollegiate Press Association (1916) and the Sooner State Press (1920).

Richard Lloyd Jones, Sr. (1873-1963), crusading editor and publisher of the *Tulsa Tribune*, editorial writer for *Collier's* Magazine, became the editorial giant of his era in Oklahoma by exposing public scandals during the 1920s and 1930s.

Jim G. Lucas (1914-1970), writer for the *Muskogee Daily Phoenix* and the *Tulsa Tribune*, top Marine combat correspondent in the Pacific during World War II, Scripps-Howard war correspondent in Korea, winner of a Pulitzer Prize and the Ernie Pyle Award.

W.R. "Bill" Martineau (1887-1970), editor and publisher of the *Oklahoma City Livestock News*, chairman of the Oklahoma City Gridiron Club for 43 years, the only life member of the Oklahoma City Press Club, Oklahoma Press Association president (1929).

Milton W. Reynolds (1833-1890), crusader in opening Oklahoma for settlement, founder of eight Nebraska, Kansas, and Oklahoma newspapers, including the oldest publication in Oklahoma, the *Edmond Sun*.

Will Rogers (1879-1935), the most widely read and influential newspaper columnist of his day, wrote his daily column "Will Rogers Says," which was published in a record 500 newspapers, helping to ease the burden of readers during the worst part of the Depression years.

— 1972

Fayette Copeland (1895-1961), journalism educator and director of the School of Journalism at the University of Oklahoma, student journalist for the *Oklahoma Daily*, recipient of the 1943 Texas Institute of Letters Award.

Earnest T. Hoberecht, Jr. (1918-1999), war correspondent in the Pacific and Asia, bureau manager and vice president for United Press and its successor, United Press International, first U.S. correspondent to land in Japan in 1945, UP general manager for Asia in 1951, and vice president in 1953, book author, publisher of four weekly newspapers in western Oklahoma.

Jenkin Lloyd Jones (1911-2004), editor and publisher of the *Tulsa Tribune*, internationally known editorial writer and columnist, served as president of the U.S. Chamber of Commerce, recipient of multiple awards, including the William Allen White Award and the Freedom Leadership Award.

Wheeler Mayo (1902-1975), founder of the *Sequoyah County Times*, writer of exposés, president of the Oklahoma Press Association (1944) and the International Conference of Weekly Newspaper Editors.

Paul Miller (1907-1991), worked with several Oklahoma newspapers, assistant general manager, and president of the Associated Press, president, chief executive, and chairman of the board of the Gannett newspaper group.

Eugene C. Pulliam (1889-1975), publisher of seven daily newspapers in Altus, Clinton, EI Reno, Mangum, Hobart, Elk City, and Alva, owner and operator of 47 newspapers, cofounder of Sigma Delta Chi Professional Journalism Society, member of the Associated Press board of directors, William Allen White Foundation trustee.

Ralph Sewell (1909-2005), Oklahoma's first national president of Sigma Delta Chi Professional Journalism Society, newsman and assistant managing editor for *The Daily Oklahoman* and *Oklahoma City Times*, mentor to young journalists.

Fred E. Tarman (1889-1981), producer of 23 state fair sweepstakes winners during 33 years of competition while editor and publisher of the *Norman Transcript*, winner of 21 awards in state competition, instrumental in founding the state's first journalism school at the University of Oklahoma.

Clement E. Trout (1891-1960), known as the "Dean of Industrial Editors," director of the journalism program at Oklahoma State University, established the nation's first industrial editing college degree and short course, helped to organize the Southwest Association of Industrial Editors and the Public Relations Society of America.

— 1973

Ben Blackstock (1924-2010), manager of the Oklahoma Press Association for more than 20 years, national president of other state press associations, political comment column writer.

Douglas Edwards (1917-1990), first major radio newsman to make the transition to television, CBS television network anchor, CBS radio broadcaster, chief of the CBS News Paris Bureau, recipient of the George Foster Peabody Award.

Raymond H. Fields (1897-1979), pioneer newsman for Pontotoc County, Indian Territory, newspaper publisher in Oklahoma, chairman of the editorial committee for the Oklahoma *American Legion Magazine* and the national *American Legion Magazine*.

D.C. "Clancy" Frost (1908-1965), publisher of the *Kiowa County Star-Review* of Hobart, winner of the Oklahoma Editorial of the Year Award and the national Herrick Editorial Award, president and long time director of the Oklahoma Press Association.

Paul Harvey (1918-2009), leading conservative political commentator and columnist, broadcaster for 462 radio stations and 126 television stations, member of the Oklahoma Hall of Fame, holder of eight honorary doctorates and eight awards from the Freedoms Foundation for his broadcasts.

Lee Hills (1906-2000), writer for the *Oklahoma City Times* and *Oklahoma News*, Pulitzer Prize winner (1956), president of Knight Newspapers, publisher of the *Detroit Free Press*, editor of the *Miami Herald*, national president of the International Press Institute, American Society of Newspaper Editors, the Associated Press Managing Editors, and Sigma Delta Chi.

Alice Lee Marriott (1910-1992), specialist in ethnology, author of 20 books and 32 major articles, Oklahoma Writer of the Year (1957), Oklahoma Hall of Fame inductee.

Joe W. McBride, Sr. (1904-1972), Oklahoma newspaper publisher, Oklahoma Hall of Fame inductee (1961), *Anadarko Daily News* publisher, president of the Oklahoma Press Association (1951).

Walker Stone (1904-1973), newspaper editor at Oklahoma State University, editor-in-chief of all Scripps-Howard newspapers, worked with the *Washington Daily News*.

— 1974

Byron L. Abernethy (1899-1959), publisher of the *Duncan Banner* (1926-59), reporter for The Associated Press, known as a "newspaperman's newspaperman."

John Cronley (1909-1972), sportswriter and editor for *The Daily Oklahoman* and the *Oklahoma City Times*, ranked among the best sports writers in accuracy, literary style, and fairness.

Alva Dopking (1908-1992), named to the Associated Press Hall of Fame, commended by U.S. officials for war reporting, Associated Press general executive for the Midwest, worked with the *Miami News-Record, Okmulgee Times-Democrat, Bartlesville Examiner,* and *Henryetta Free-Lance*.

Norris G. Henthorne, Sr. (1891-1962), bookkeeper, then president and editor of the *Tulsa Daily World*, community, state, and national leader, president of the Oklahoma Press Association (1934), member of the Oklahoma Hall of Fame, served as a director of the Oklahoma Historical Society.

Frank McGee (1921-1974) broadcaster for KGFF Shawnee (1940), WKY-TV Oklahoma City (1950), and WSFA-TV Montgomery, Alabama (1955), worked with the NBC national television network, recipient of the 1968 Emmy.

Jack Morris (1921-2010), Oklahoma's first winner of the Edward R. Murrow Award (1966), documentary producer, broadcaster, Tulsa correspondent for the United Press, served with the Armed Forces Radio during World War II, news director of KTUL-TV (1954) and KTEW-TV (1970).

Ned Shepler (1896-1967), publisher of *The Lawton Constitution* and the *Lawton Morning Press*, Oklahoma Hall of Fame member, served on the Southern Newspaper Publishers Association Board of Directors, president of the Associated Press Editors of Oklahoma, president of the Oklahoma Press Association (1931).

Vance H. Trimble (1913-), first state journalist to win the "triple crown" in national journalism awards (1960)—a Pulitzer Prize, the Raymond Clapper Memorial Award, and the Sigma Delta Chi award for his series on nepotism in Congress, author of bestselling books and many true detective stories, former editor of the *Kentucky Post* in Covington, managing editor of the *Houston Press*.

Harrington Wimberly (1900-1978), editor and publisher of the *Altus Times-Democrat* (1929-66), publisher of the *Duncan Banner*, manager of Eugene Pulliam organization newspapers, Oklahoma director of the Office of War Information during World War II, president of the Oklahoma Press Association (1937), the Oklahoma Newspaper Foundation and the Southern Newspaper Publishers Association.

— 1975

Victor F. Barnett (1894-1968), managing editor, advertising manager, and associate editor at the *Tulsa Tribune*, charter member of the National Conference of Editorial Writers, member of the American Society of Newspaper Editors.

Tams Bixby, Jr. (1891-1970), editor and publisher of the *Muskogee Daily Phoenix* and *Times-Democrat*, president of KBIX Radio station in Muskogee, publisher of the *Springfield News and Leader Press*.

James J. Craddock (1904-1974), Oklahoma Press Association president (1948), publisher of the *Weatherford News*, which won sweepstakes in Oklahoma State Fair competitions and Oklahoma Heritage Society contests.

Dr. Rex Harlow (1892-1993), author, founder, and president of the American Council on Public Relations (1940), pioneer in establishing the Public Relations Society of America, the Public Relations Department of Stanford University, and the *Public Relations Journal*.

Earl C. Hull (1895-1971), longtime leader in the world of commercial radio broadcasting, established WKY Radio in Oklahoma City, operating the station for nearly 20 years, founder of the radio station WHLD.

William D. Little, Sr. (1888-1966), winner of many editorial writing awards, staff member, editor, and publisher for the *Ada Evening News*, community newspaper advocate.

Edward K. Livermore, Sr. (1918-2014), first Oklahoman to serve as president of the National Newspaper Association, president of the Oklahoma Press Association (1959-60), owner and co-owner of several state newspapers, owner of the Sapulpa radio station.

Lea M. Nichols (1888-1963), the first Oklahoman to serve as president of the National Editorial Association, nationally famous editor and publisher of the *Bristow Record* (1905-1946), president of the Oklahoma Press Association (1930).

Otis W. Sullivant (1902-1974), political reporter and columnist for *The Daily Oklahoman* and the *Oklahoma City Times*, covered 15 national political conventions and 10 campaigns for president, governor, and the U. S. Senate.

— 1976

Lou S. Allard (1909-1974), editor and co-publisher of the *Drumright Derrick* and *Drumright Journal* (1930-74), served in the state Legislature for 24 years, co-authored present-day open meetings law, honored by the Oklahoma City Press Club and Sigma Delta Chi.

Jack Bell (1904-1975), reporter and city editor for *The Daily Oklahoman* (1925-1937), author of four books, chief political writer for the Associated Press (1937-1969), political columnist for Gannett Newspapers (1969-1975).

John Casey (1898-deceased), founder of the national Future Journalists of America at the University of Oklahoma, writer for the *Knoxville* (Iowa) *Express*, advertising manager of the (Tokyo) *Japan Advertiser*, associate editor of the *Trans-Pacific Magazine*, market editor of the *Nashville Tennessean*, served on the Schools of Journalism Committee of the National Editorial Association.

Gerald "Cowboy" Curtin (1907-1965), country newspaper editor and publisher, managing editor of the *Guthrie Daily Leader*, sportswriter for the *Oklahoma News*, editor and publisher of the *Watonga Republican*, president of the Oklahoma Press Association (1952).

John F. Easley (1872-1956), owner of the *Daily Ardmoreite*, established radio station KVSO of Ardmore, recipient of the Distinguished Service Award from the University of Oklahoma (1952), Oklahoma Hall of Fame inductee.

Foster Harris (1903-1978), author, freelance writer, helped establish the University of Oklahoma professional writing program in 1937, worked on *The Daily Oklahoman*, the *Wes-Tex Oil and Gas News* in Amarillo, the Western World oil and mining newspaper in Fort Worth, the *Petroleum Daily* in Dallas, the *Fort Worth Press* in Texas, and the *Des Moines Register* in Iowa.

Hattie Mae Lachenmeyer (1901-1978), co-editor and co-publisher of seven daily newspapers in Oklahoma, Texas, and Louisiana, recipient of the 1949 Theta Sigma Phi Matrix Table Award as the female journalist who rendered the greatest service to Oklahoma.

O.H. Lachenmeyer (1893-1953), co-editor and co-publisher of seven daily newspapers in Oklahoma, Texas, and Louisiana, president of the Oklahoma Press Association (1947), chairman of the Oklahoma Fish and Game Commission.

Bruce Palmer (1909-1973), national president of the Radio-Television News Editors Association, worked with The Associated Press, *The Daily Oklahoman,* and the *Oklahoma City Times*, news director of WKY Radio, U.S. information officer in Ceylon, news director of KWTV, news director of the Public Relations Department of Lowe Runkle.

George H. Evans (1873-1954), editor and publisher of the *Chickasha Daily Express* for 50 years, contributing founder of the Oklahoma College for Women at Chickasha, president of the Oklahoma Press Association (1907).

James J. Kilpatrick (1920-2010), nationally syndicated columnist, national television network political commentator, author, recipient of the University of Missouri School of Journalism Medal of Honor for Distinguished Service in Journalism (1953), chairman of the National Conference of Editorial Writers, recipient of the Outstanding Editorial Writer Award of The Society of Professional Journalists, Sigma Delta Chi (1954).

Wauhillau Lahay (1909-1992), Washington columnist for Scripps-Howard newspapers, first Oklahoman to serve as president of the Washington Press Club, first woman on the governing board of Scripps-Howard Broadcasting, reporter and columnist for *The Oklahoman*, broadcaster for WKY Radio.

Richard Gamble Miller (1890-1970), reporter for *The Daily Oklahoman* and *Oklahoma City Times* (1920-68), columnist of "The Smoking Room" by RGM (1935-1968), author of *See and Know Oklahoma,* which sold 175,000 copies.

 **Harmon Phillips** (1904-1975), *Tulsa Tribune* newsman, starting as a reporter (1927), then to city editor (1937), managing editor (1944), executive editor (1968), and assistant publisher (1974), founder of the Tulsa Press Club and its president for three terms, two-time president of the Oklahoma Press Managing Editors.

 **H. Milt Phillips** (1898-1979), publisher of the *Seminole Producer*, served as president, chairman, or commander of 20 civic, professional, and veterans' organizations, editor for the *Oklahoma Legionnaire*, served as Department Adjutant for the American Legion, served as president (1953) and treasurer of the Oklahoma Press Association.

 **Corbin Mark Sarchet** (1877-1971), freelance journalist, called the "dean of Oklahoma newsmen," covered the constitutional convention (1907) for *The Daily Oklahoman*, published the *Shamrock Brogue*, credited at the time with writing more feature and news stories about Oklahoma than any other journalist.

 **Frosty Troy** (1933-2017), winner of 15 state and national awards for journalistic excellence, worked with *The Tulsa Tribune* (1957-70), named Oklahoma Newsman of the Year, owner and publisher of the *Oklahoma Observer*.

 **Paul R. Wade** (1907-1972) publisher of the *Elk City Daily News* (1934-72), which won three state fair sweepstakes and was once selected as the best newspaper in the Southwest by the U.S. Soil Conservation Service.

— **1978**

 **Edward Austin** (1897-1975), worked on newspapers in Frederick, Milwaukee, Oklahoma City, and Chicago; member of the Scripps-Howard newspaper organization in Cleveland (1928), managing editor for the *San Diego Evening Tribune* and the *Morning Union* of Copley Newspapers, executive editor of all 17 Copley newspapers.

 **Harold R. Belknap** (1904-1975), contributor, editor, and publisher for the *Norman Transcript*, trustee for the Oklahoma Newspaper Foundation, president of the Oklahoma Press Association (1973).

 **Edgar T. Bell** (1893-1972), advertising manager of the *Oklahoma Farmer-Stockman*, general manager for the Oklahoma Publishing Company and WKY Radio, station manager for KTOK, vice president and general manager of Oklahoma City's second television station, KWTV.

Fred G. Cowles (1866-1949), newspaperman for 63 years, publisher of the *McAlester News Capital* (1918-49), devoted community member.

Travis Hensley (1851-1944), founder of the *El Reno Democrat*, established *The Westside Democrat of Enid* in the Cherokee Outlet the day the territory opened for settlement, established *Hensley's Magazine* and the *People's Press* in El Reno, contributing founder of the Oklahoma Press Association, served in both houses of the Oklahoma Legislature, Oklahoma Hall of Fame inductee.

George Hill (1915-1994), worked with the *Ardmore Morning Democrat, Ada Bulletin*, and *Johnston County Capital-Democrat*, co-publisher and editor of the *Capital-Democrat*, publisher of the *Coalgate Record-Register*, president of the Oklahoma Press Association (1956-57).

Donald W. Reynolds (1906-1993), publisher of 31 daily newspapers in eight states, including the *Fort Smith Southwest Times, Okmulgee Times, Bartlesville Examiner, Blackwell Journal-Tribune, Chickasha Daily Express, Guthrie Daily Leader, Pawhuska Journal-Capital, Guymon Daily Herald, Pauls Valley Democrat, Wewoka Times, Holdenville Daily News*, and *Henryetta Daily Democrat*.

Ernest J. "Ernie" Schultz (1930-2017), worked with KGEO-TV in Enid, now KOCO-TV, and KTVY, formerly WKY-TV, in Oklahoma City as a reporter-photographer and director, national president of the Radio Television News Directors Association, president of the Oklahoma Associated Press Broadcasters and the Oklahoma City professional chapter of the Society of Professional Journalists.

Travis Walsh (1924-1976), worked with the *Tulsa Daily World* as Oklahoma State Capitol and Washington correspondent, editorial writer, and managing editor, president of the Oklahoma Associated Press Managing Editors, president of the Eastern Oklahoma Chapter of the Society of Professional Journalists, recipient of the Beachy Musselman Award of the Oklahoma Press Association.

— 1979

Harry S. Culver (1922-2005), international vice president for the Newspaper Guild, secretary-treasurer and president of the Wire Service Guild, worked with the *Anadarko Daily News* and *Shawnee News-Star*, head of United Press International Statehouse Bureau, recipient of two state and one national award for excellence in governmental and education reporting.

Phil Dessauer (1918-1997), the second Oklahoman to serve as national president of the Society of Professional Journalists, Sigma Delta Chi, worked on *The Daily Oklahoman*, the *Oklahoma City Times*, and United Press, capitol correspondent, editorial writer, associate editor, columnist, and managing editor for the *Tulsa Daily World*.

Ray J. Dyer (1899-1992), president (1955) and manager of the Oklahoma Press Association, worked on newspapers in Kansas and Missouri, telegraph editor for the *Oklahoma City Times*, managing editor of *Oklahoma News*, editor and publisher of the *EI Reno Tribune*.

John Fischer (1910-1978), worked with *Harper's Magazine* as editor (1944-52), editor-in-chief (1953-67), and contributing editor (1967-78), worked on *The Daily Oklahoman* (1928-32), the United Press (1933-35), and The Associated Press Washington Bureau (1935-37);,Rhodes Scholar, author of four published books.

S. Edward Lee (1886-1982), founder and publisher of the *Harper County Journal* at Buffalo, developer of civic and youth programs in his county and state, president of the Oklahoma Press Association (1942), helped to pass the "honest mistake" law in Oklahoma to protect the press.

Charles Long (1938-2008), news editor and editor of *The Quill*, *Who's Who in America* listee, author of *With Optimism for the Morrow*, editor of *Sooner Magazine* (1963-66), worked with the *San Angelo Standard-Times* (1961-62) and the *Norman Transcript* (1962-63).

Earl H. Richert (1914-2005), worked with Scripps-Howard Newspapers for 43 years as copy boy for *Oklahoma News* (1936-37), editor and editor-in-chief for all 18 Scripps-Howard newspapers, Scripps-Howard's youngest editor for the *Evansville Press*.

THE 1980s
the bust and boom years can't damper journalistic history

While Oklahoma was going through the oil bust years of the 1980s, the Oklahoma Journalism Hall of Fame was inducting new members who were civil rights activists, philanthropists, authors, and Oklahoma Territory pioneers.

E.L. Goodwin, editor and publisher of the *Oklahoma Eagle* in Tulsa, was among the first inductees of the 1980s. Goodwin won fame for his lifelong campaign for civil and human rights.

"His editorial voice often was neither popular nor safe, but he fought for equality with tenacity and courage," his Hall of Fame biography reads.

Goodwin was joined that year by Jacques DeLier, president and general manager of KWTV in Oklahoma City. DeLier has attended the induction ceremony every year since his induction. By the 50th anniversary, DeLier will be nearing his 101st birthday.

DeLier is one of many pioneers of Oklahoma journalism and literature who became members in the 1980s. Other members include Oklahoma Territory publisher Frank Hilton Greer and Leslie Gordon Niblack, publisher of the influential *Guthrie Daily Leader,* and famed writer Ralph Ellison, author of *Invisible Man* that won the National Book Award in 1953. Others such as Harry E. Heath, N. Beachey Musselman, Hall of Fame founder Ray Tassin, and Vivian Vahlberg would join them in 1983. However, Vahlberg and fellow inductee Allan W. Cromley couldn't attend the ceremony because a February snowstorm grounded them in Washington, D.C. The ceremony was later moved to the spring. Also included in the decade's classes were Jack Bickham, who wrote 61 published novels and was a renowned educator and writer, and Dick Hefton, a longtime publisher and editor who was promoted to an Air Force brigadier general.

A journalist and renowned philanthropist became a member at the end of the decade. Edith Kinney Gaylord, inducted in 1989, became known not only for her journalism career but for launching the Ethics and Excellence in Journalism Foundation that has benefited thousands of journalists and journalism organizations. She was posthumously inducted into the Oklahoma Hall of Fame in 2012.

The members who joined in the 1980s would leave legacies that will continue to influence future generations long past the 50th anniversary.

George Cornell, AP's national religion writer (1988 inductee). Date unknown. AP Photo/ Corporate Archives.

On March 4, 1868, Jesse Chisholm, Cherokee, a trailblazer, sickened and died. April 15, 1949, *The Daily Oklahoman*. Al McLaughlin photo. Courtesy of the Oklahoma Historical Society.

Photograph used for a story in *The Daily Oklahoman*, September 9, 1947. Al McLaughlin photo. Courtesy of the Oklahoma Historical Society.

JACQUES DELIER
from war hero to journalism pioneer
By Emily Siddiqui, Student Editor

Raoul Jacques "Jack" DeLier was a war hero before traveling the country to sell motion pictures for Universal Studios. Then a job offer changed his life and propelled him into a distinguished career, one which earned him induction into the Oklahoma Journalism Hall of Fame in 1980.

As I interviewed him in his Oklahoma City home filled with pictures of his family, DeLier remembered back to the 1950s when Independent Theatres President Henry Griffing offered him a job at KWTV-Channel 9. Just weeks after the Oklahoma City station first went on the air, he became national sales manager on January 8, 1954.

"I had no broadcast experience whatsoever," DeLier said, laughing. Initially, he had no idea what he was selling or who his customers were. He went on to become general sales manager, station manager, general manager, and then president of Griffin Television. He was president of the station when he retired in 1982.

"That's what you call working your way up," he said.

Of course, even as a young broadcast journalist, leadership was nothing new to DeLier. He was student council president and captain of the baseball team in high school. In college, he was president of his fraternity. He would later serve as president of many nonprofits and institutions.

"I was always in charge of something," he told me. "I relished responsibility."

At 100 years old, he has a sharp memory and speaks with careful attention to detail. DeLier is legally blind, yet still looked me in the eyes as he shared stories in his deep, distinctive voice. Due to a vascular condition he lost his left leg in 2014, but he gets around well in a wheelchair. He showed me his war medals and a few of his many awards, all of which

he is humble about. I looked closely at a seaside painting in his living room—the small signature at the bottom revealed he was also a talented artist. He reminded me that he gives credit to God for all of his blessings in life.

DeLier was born in 1919 in Minot, North Dakota, but grew up in Omaha, Nebraska. There, he attended a Catholic preparatory school. He then went to the University of Oklahoma on a football scholarship, only to suffer a severe leg injury, which forced him to forego that dream.

He enrolled in journalism courses and majored in history, but never actually graduated from OU. Instead, he joined the U.S. Army Air Corps, learning to fly the newly built Martin B-26 Marauder and soon becoming a flight instructor. That same year, he married Barbara Ann, who would be his devoted wife for more than six decades.

Then came the attack on Pearl Harbor in December 1941. Captain DeLier flew 65 combat missions in England and France, but not without cost to him personally. On June 13, 1944, his plane was hit by antiaircraft fire while flying over Normandy. Steel shattered and hit DeLier in the face; two fellow crew members were killed. For his injuries, DeLier received a Purple Heart. He has also received the Air Medal, the Distinguished Flying Cross, and, most recently, the French Legion of Honor.

His son, Michael, would later join his father in being awarded the Purple Heart for injuries he suffered during the Vietnam War. Michael also followed him in broadcast management and shares DeLier's passion for sports, especially golf.

In 1959, DeLier attended graduate school at Harvard to further his education in management development. His daughter, Michelin, also excelled academically, earning a law degree from OU and a master's degree at Stanford University.

DeLier could be considered a KWTV historian when talking about the changes broadcast journalism has seen over the decades. Fewer than a dozen people occupied the newsroom in the beginning. When he left, he said, about 70 people were in the news department.

DeLier remembered working with other Hall of Fame members, such as Lola Hall and Jan Lovell. Even as general manager, DeLier was never above personally taking phone calls, no matter who was on the line—whether it was a distressed citizen asking the station not to run a family member's suicide story or angry callers expressing their political views.

For nearly 50 years, he has attended every Hall of Fame induction ceremony, sitting at the same honorary table provided to him. He's thankful that such an honor exists for those outstanding contributors to our state's history.

"I think it's a beautiful thing to have, to reward not only broadcast journalism, but all journalism, in our area … [and] to honor the people who really worked hard at journalism and tried to do what journalists are supposed to do."

From left, Jacques DeLier, Dewey F. Bartlett, and Henry Bellmon. Photo taken circa 1975.

Captain Jacques DeLier flew 65 combat missions during World War II. He has received the Air Medal, the Distinguished Flying Cross, the French Legion of Honor, and a Purple Heart. Photo taken circa 1942.

VIVIAN VAHLBERG
home with the most powerful in Washington
By Vivian Vahlberg, 1983 Inductee

Everyone in my seventh-grade carpool to Oklahoma City's Taft Junior High School wanted to try out for the school newspaper. I didn't.

I had no interest in getting my hands dirty with printers' ink. When I learned that being on newspaper staff meant writing the stories, my attitude changed. I tried out and, despite being initially clueless, was chosen editor, the start of an amazing career in and around journalism.

Little did I realize then where journalism would take me. First, it took me to Washington, D.C. where I got to report for *The Daily Oklahoman* (and then also for the *Colorado Springs Sun*) for 12 years, writing about whatever happened in Washington that affected Oklahoma or Colorado more than other states—from the actions of the states' congressional delegations to Native American affairs; defense, agriculture, and energy policy; campaign finance; and U.S. Supreme Court cases.

Among the notables I covered were U.S. Senators Henry Bellmon and David Boren, U.S. Senators and presidential candidates Fred Harris and Gary Hart, and U.S. House Speaker Carl Albert. I even ventured outside D.C. occasionally, writing about Oklahomans working on North Sea oil rigs off the coast of Norway, national political conventions, and a presidential trip.

One of my first assignments was to cover the all-male National Press Club's 1971 vote to finally admit women as members. How amazing that, 11 years later, I would become the club's first woman president, helping this important Washington institution put its discriminatory past behind it. This was considered such a milestone that President Ronald Reagan swore me in, braving picketers from the National Organization for Women who saluted my selection while protesting Reagan's opposition to the Equal Rights Amendment.

My year as president in 1982 was jam-packed with challenges, including presiding over 70 hour-long luncheon programs that were always broadcast live nationally, and sometimes internationally. As president, I hosted our high-profile speakers at a pre-luncheon reception and then presided over the luncheon program, introducing and questioning the featured guests. Speakers included many heads of state, among them India's Indira Gandhi, Pakistan's Muhammad Zia-ul-Haq, Egypt's Hosni Mubarak, the Philippines' Ferdinand Marcos, the queen of the Netherlands, media giants Al Neuharth and Dan Rather, and entertainment greats such as Francis Ford Coppola and Gene Kelly.

The speakers always made news, but I remember the personal things—like how Queen Beatrix of the Netherlands considered her luncheon appearance so important she spent 90 minutes with me beforehand. Or, Indian Prime Minister Indira Gandhi's nervousness when her son got stuck in the elevator of the National Press Building, which had been undergoing a massive reconstruction. Or, Philippine President Ferdinand Marcos' disingenuous reply when I asked about corruption in his country: "You must be thinking of some other country."

Through my involvement with the Press Club, I came to see what a difference nonprofit organizations make, helping news professionals do together what they cannot do alone—fight First Amendment battles, develop new skills, promote diversity in staffing and news coverage, and jointly address financial and technological challenges buffeting news businesses.

So, when my family and I moved to Chicago, Illinois in the 1980s, my career shifted from doing journalism to working in the nonprofit sector on programs affecting journalism. Sometimes I ran programs, as executive director of the Society of Professional Journalists and as managing director of the Media Management Center at Northwestern University. Other times I led foundation investments in journalism-related initiatives, such as when I was director of Journalism Programs at McCormick Tribune Foundation and manager of the Community News Matters program at The Chicago Community Trust. Along the way, I also

Vivian Vahlberg, right, met many famous people during her newspaper career. Here she is pictured with India Prime Minister Indira Gandhi.

conducted research on community news needs and Internet news usage.

Fortunately, in recent years, the path has led me back to Oklahoma City twice a year, to consult about journalism grant-making with the Ethics and Excellence in Journalism Foundation.

It's always great to return home!

SHAWNEE NEWS-STAR
the Hall of Fame newsroom in the 1980s
By Joe Hight, 2013 Inductee

In a small newsroom, the *Shawnee News-Star* was filled with future Hall of Famers when I worked there in the 1980s.

I worked there twice, between a short stint at *The Lawton Constitution* and *Morning Press* where I also worked with Hall of Famers Ted Ralston,

Paul McClung, and Jeff Dixon in the newsroom. I also worked there with columnist and author Jon Talton.

But the *News-Star's* newsroom was special. It was a close-knit group who did things such as play paper baseball with each other during lulls in the evening, endured a flood in the newsroom and many calls from a publisher who drank too much, and ate and spent time with each other often, even outside the newsroom.

Until I was working on this book, I hadn't realized how special they were. The newsroom was led by managing editor Jim Bradshaw when I was there. Bradshaw, who spent most of his career in Shawnee, was known as a fiery journalist, but who was a sensitive boss with a great sense of humor. Every night we would hear his stories, including how he was once thrown into jail by the sheriff because of his reporting.

In 1995, Bradshaw was the first of that group to be inducted into the Hall of Fame. But five others from that same newsroom would join him. Five of the six spent most of their careers at the *News-Star.* Sports Editor Roy Angel was the first in 2000. Mike McCormick, who later became executive editor, followed in 2005. I, who might be considered the group's short timer, would follow in 2013. Photographer Ed Blochowiak was inducted a year later. And, Virginia Bradshaw, one of the most pleasant and persistent reporters I've ever known, joined her husband in the Hall of Fame in 2016. I suspect others such as Fred Fehr, who followed Angel as a longtime sports editor and worked in the same newsroom, will become part of this Hall of Fame group someday.

The newsroom was so talented that it won the Oklahoma Press Association's coveted Sweepstakes Award for the first time while I was there as city editor under Jim Bradshaw.

I've been fortunate to meet and work with many great journalists, including those at *The Oklahoman.* But I now realize how fortunate I was to start with some of the finest early in my career.

ALLAN CROMLEY
thriving in the greatest generation of journalists
By Ed Kelley, 2003 Inductee

He had a bearing, did Allan Cromley, of a man made for Washington, D.C. in an era made for men who came to town at the top of their game and stayed long enough to have witnessed the great shifts in American journalism—and thrived all the while in it.

He and his wife Marian, nine months pregnant with their first child, arrived by car in steamy Washington from Oklahoma City in June 1953, not sure how long the stay would be but determined to make the most of it there.

Turned out "there," in terms of Al Cromley's career in Washington for *The Oklahoman*, lasted another 43 years.

Along the way he covered what seemed like a jillion stories for *The Oklahoman* and its sister paper, *The Oklahoma City Times*. Some of them were as big as they get: a presidential assassination, the space program (his publisher, Hall of Famer Edward King Gaylord, loved science and thus orbiting in the heavens), political conventions (19 of them), a presidential summit in the Soviet Union. And the bread and butter of smaller, more mundane stories: Oklahoma's congressional delegation particularly, but also the machinations of official Washington and how they affected the folks back home.

At the time he arrived in Washington, his peers were men like him, top-shelf reporters who first made their mark at their home papers. They were members of the Greatest Generation who had postponed college to go to war for Uncle Sam, in his case in the Battle of the Bulge.

He was ambitious, in ways not unlike the other ambitious people in government and politics who helped turn post-war Washington from a sleepy southern town into the news capital of the world. It helped too that Al Cromley looked the part—tall and handsome, with a head full of preternatural gray-then-white hair. He was mistaken from time to time as a member of the fraternity he covered—specifically, the Senate. Colleagues in the home office called him "the senior senator from OPUBCO."

As proof: A national magazine years ago wanted to portray what the Senate would look like if its gender breakdown at the time—98 men and two women—were reversed. So, it found 98 women for the photo it wanted and needed two men who could pass for senators to play the part. "What about Al Cromley?" someone asked. And in the photo he appeared.

He could have passed for a senator, but he wasn't one of them. His reporting often chafed the high and mighty. Early on, it was Robert S. Kerr, "the uncrowned king of the Senate." Then there was an occasional spat with Senator Henry Bellmon or on the House side, Carl Albert, who later was Speaker of the House. As it was he outlasted all of them.

Working with him, as I did for four years at the end of his career, was illuminating. He could write any kind of story. But he wanted the verbiage, particularly for his Sunday column, to be just right. And even after four decades in the business Al Cromley would literally pace the floor of his small office in the National Press Building, mentally searching for exactly the right word or phrase to make his point.

He came to work in coat and tie, not just because he was of that generation but because he knew he represented more than just himself. His example to me, without saying so: as *The Oklahoman's* person in Washington, you represent the paper and its owners. And to many people encountered on a daily basis, you might be the only person they've ever met from Oklahoma City or Oklahoma. First impressions never meant more than in Washington.

And he impressed many.

Cromley remains one of the few to ever have served as president of both the National Press Club and the prestigious Gridiron Club. He was inducted into the Hall of Fame in 1983.

He began working part-time upon turning 65 and worked another nine years, until 1996.

Al Cromley takes a break from his work covering America's early space program in the 1960s. The picture was taken at Cape Canaveral and accompanied the news story *The Washington Post* ran after Cromley died in 2011.

He had experienced it all.

He started on a manual typewriter at a time when newspapers—morning and afternoon—were king and television news just a blip. Desktop computers eventually came along, then rudimentary laptops. News via the Internet was birthed as he called it quits.

It was quite the ride for a man who was made for the role he played—and played well for so long.

DR. HARRY E. HEATH, JR.
'But it's Harry'
By Terry Clark, 2000 Inductee

"The man who taught Oklahoma's journalists" was the Oklahoma Press Association's front-page headline in the *Oklahoma Publisher* when Dr. Harry Heath, Jr. died.

The paper "turned" the column rules, an old journalism tradition, with the comment, "because we mourn the loss of our colleague, mentor, and most of all, friend."

Everybody in Oklahoma journalism knew Heath, the dean of Oklahoma journalism. The seemingly frail, lean man with a gray inverted pyramid beard and hawk nose, Heath was the energetic embodiment of an Oklahoma journalist and scholar.

Heath served as head of the Oklahoma State University journalism program from 1967 to 1982 and then taught full-time until 1986. But his influence on Oklahoma journalists went far beyond the Stillwater campus. He was inducted into the Hall of Fame in 1983.

He never stopped writing, including his 30-year column, "Heath's Critique," every month in the *Oklahoma Publisher* that made him a friend of journalists in virtually every newspaper in the state. Being mentioned in his column was an affirmation of quality and worthiness. He also wrote for national publications and several books, on sports and broadcast writing, poetry and more, plus numerous educational booklets and pamphlets for journalists.

"I wish I'd written that" was the highest praise he gave many journalists, either in his column or as he traveled the state conducting educational clinics, as a refresher and especially for beginning journalists at smaller papers for the OPA.

Traveling with him across the state to conduct those clinics was an adventure in ideas. His apartment was strewn with stacks of countless manila folders full of journalism examples and ideas. He would bring enough material with him for a week's workshop instead of a day's focus. On the drives, there would be Frank Sinatra on the radio, or he'd be whistling, or telling stories. There would be constant conversation about the need for excellence in journalism, no matter the size of publication or type of program, and that was his passion.

Heath began his journalism career on his school newspaper at Tulsa Central High School. He also taught at The University of Tulsa, Iowa State University, and the University of Florida.

When teaching writing, or anything connected with journalism, he knew what he was talking about. He served as both sports and general assignment reporter for the *Tulsa Tribune* and *Tulsa World*, news editor for the central division (Chicago) for NBC, and writer and producer for WOI-TV in Ames, Iowa. In addition, he handled public relations duties at The University of Iowa and the U.S. Army.

Under his tenure, the OSU journalism school grew from 200 students as majors to more than 750. But the growth was more than numbers; it reflected the professional development of the curriculum and caliber of the faculty he brought to OSU.

He constantly worked to improve journalism throughout Oklahoma. He provided motivating programs to other groups such as the Industrial Editors organization, Women in Communications, Public Relations Student Society, high school journalism advisers, and the Society of Professional Journalists.

His reputation went beyond Oklahoma as a speaker for numerous national and international conventions and chairing national committees for the Association of Education in Journalism.

In addition to his induction into the Hall of Fame, he was the only Oklahoman to be twice named Friend of Journalism by Oklahoma's Society of Professional Journalists. OPA honored him with both the Milt Phillips Award and the Beachy Musselman Award.

When he was critically injured in the car wreck that would lead to his death in 1996, the late Lawrence Gibbs, then editor of the *Stillwater*

Harry E. Heath, Jr. in Oklahoma State University's Old Central building. Photo by a journalism student in Photo I class. 1973.

Harry Heath, Jr. (center) with fellow Hall of Fame members Jimmie Baker (left) and James R. Bellatti. Date unknown.

News Press, called The Associated Press' Oklahoma bureau. AP told him it didn't carry car wreck news. Gibbs replied, "But it's Harry."

AP ran the story.

MONTEZ TJADEN

private woman to public legend in Tulsa

By Ralph Schaefer, 2017 Inductee

Montez Tjaden was the consummate public relations professional and leader that helped set a positive economic growth pattern in Oklahoma. She worked with and around everyone, from political leaders including President Richard M. Nixon and Senator Robert S. Kerr to top-level business leaders.

Despite her high public profile, Tjaden was a private person from Lindsborg, Kansas, who served in the U.S. Navy and was national president of American Women in Radio and Television (AWRT).

Tjaden worked with officials to bring President Nixon to Tulsa to dedicate the McClellan-Kerr Arkansas River Navigation System waterway. She worked with Oklahoma's U.S. Senator Robert S. Kerr as he purchased television stations throughout the country, and she is credited with helping put Tulsa's KRMG Radio and Oklahoma City's KWTV on the air.

Steve Turnbo, Schnake Turnbo Frank chairman emeritus, recalled his experiences with the PR legend, who was inducted into the Hall of Fame in 1988.

"Montez came to Tulsa to join Advertising Incorporated (Ad Inc.) from Oklahoma City's Channel 9 where she served as promotions director," Turnbo said. "I was The University of Tulsa Sports Information Director in 1970 and was hired to work with Tjaden to coordinate the waterway dedication, an event that would draw an estimated 30,000 people to the area. Montez and I worked on many exciting projects. She was known nationally and internationally.

"Tjaden was involved with the Navy League for Naval Officers or Commanders. She knew how to deal with the media, was a good writer and a wonderful lady," he said. "But she was tough. If you were late for work, you were told about being tardy." She was strict, disciplined, and had a high work ethic.

Tjaden saw Senator Kerr's leadership first-hand. These are two of many stories she could tell.

Kerr was going to Peoria, Illinois to dedicate a television station he had recently purchased. Meeting Kerr at the airport, Tjaden told him about striking cameramen and asked if they should use the station's back door. Kerr said he would use the front door.

Arriving, Kerr took off his hat, walked up to a picketer and said, "My name is Bob Kerr. What's yours?"

The man answered. Kerr said, "We will talk about this strike," then carried on a conversation with him.

Montez Tjaden helped put Tulsa's KRMG Radio and Oklahoma City's KWTV television stations on the air. Her career also included working with newspapers, in public relations, and serving in the U.S. Navy.

An Associated Press photographer took the picture of the two men shaking hands that was carried in about 50 newspapers across the country.

Another story involved Tulsa-area community leaders debating the value of the proposed McClellan-Kerr waterway at a Claremore church when Kerr arrived. Kerr walked to the front and said, "Let's start this meeting. Turn to page 346 and sing, 'Shall We Gather at The River?'"

"Such was Kerr's leadership," Tjaden said.

"Montez Tjaden's legacy might be the waterway or that she worked with Senator Bob Kerr," Turnbo said. "It might be she was the national AWRT president. It's hard to pick one over the other.

"Her real legacy is she was a leader in the 1970s, a bit ahead of her time for female leadership in this city [Tulsa]. I don't know if leaders at that time recognized her leadership, but I know they listened to and respected her."

ROBERT B. ALLEN
the second act from any burg in Oklahoma
By Ed Kelley, 2003 Inductee

Consider, if you would, the second act of Bob Allen's journalistic life, after he left the familiar confines of his small hometown to be a big city reporter, in this case a reporter who did more past middle age than most of his counterparts—those whipper-snapper Baby Boomers—could muster over entire careers.

He helped edit the *Cushing Daily Citizen* until age 49, when *The Oklahoman and Times* hired him as an editorial writer. Write he could, but he was a bit out of sorts, in a polite way, with the paper's conservative stance. So, after a year, Edward King Gaylord found him a home as a roving reporter—with an expense account and company car—on his state staff. This, at a time when the paper covered Oklahoma border to border, was a big deal. And for the next 15 years until retirement the byline of

Robert B. (Bolivar) Allen was a "Page One" staple, usually accompanied by a dateline from—you name it—just about any burg in Oklahoma.

Naturally he was most at home on the front page, befitting his "Front-Page" mien.

First, the look. Classic Allen: Accompanying the mustache and an early Beatle-like haircut was the sartorial splendor of a light-colored suit, striped shirt, wide tie, loafers, maybe even socks, and in the hot Oklahoma sun, a pair of mirror shades. On the first finger of his right hand was a garish ring, made just for him by a prison inmate, a "peckerwood" who admired Allen's work as if he were a law-abiding reader in the suburbs.

He smoked, a lot, and drank, well, a lot. Fingers floated across a typewriter's keyboard, but his work shone brightest when he dictated his stories to colleagues in the office. Inside a motel room on deadline with a landline phone in hand, he composed the sentences and paragraphs in his head, flipping through notes. "Knock it, Sue," he occasionally would instruct his wife, a frequent traveling companion. "Knock it" meant for Sue to add a bit more ice and Jim Beam to the motel plastic cup as he worked his magic.

Details and color for his stories occasionally were secured through a technique that amused colleagues but was quite effective. Allen would tell a source that he was desperate for their help, hinting that he was in trouble with the home office and he really, really needed to get the story if he were to stay employed.

What a ruse! On many days Allen was the best reporter at the paper and maybe in the state.

And he could make the toughest assignments look easy, through gravitas, charm and guile. I was a witness to Allen at his best.

The office got word one evening that a riot had erupted at the state reformatory at Granite. I arrived in time to help with *The Oklahoman's* story for the final edition, then remained awake overnight and through the following day to file and update for the four editions of the *Oklahoma City Times*, the afternoon paper. Allen arrived at about 6:00 p.m. and suddenly, the disturbance was over. And to get his story he instructed everyone gathered in the warden's office to stand along the wall so that he could go to each of them with his questions. Each waited his turn, like obedient children.

A bit later, Sue drove them to the nearby Quartz Mountain Lodge so he could dictate the play story for the next morning.

Another time, Allen was back in Cushing, babysitting his grandson on a rare Friday afternoon off. A young editor decided to dispatch him anyway, this time to the bizarre killing of a high school football coach by his assistant. Allen drove 50 miles to the murder scene in Bixby. His interviews secured, he dictated 40 inches off the top of his head, then drove back to Cushing in time for dinner.

The hint here is that while Allen could cover anything—and he did, from the A&M regents to beauty pageants—his forte was the human condition, as in how Oklahomans could act in the worst possible ways toward their fellow citizens.

This made him a frequent presence in prisons, particularly in McAlester. His reporting career coincided with the final executions of the 1960s before a halt to them for a couple decades. Allen was at the penitentiary for the last one, in 1966, of two-time killer James French. After the electrocution Allen was about to call the office when French's body was wheeled nearby. "French wanted you to have this," a prison guard said, handing Allen an envelope. The letter inside was written by French specifically for Allen, explaining his state of mind just before the state of Oklahoma executed him.

This was the effect that a conversation or encounter with Allen had on many Oklahomans, from the most despicable to the most reputable. His occasional shtick—I'm a broken-down reporter on the verge of being fired—belied a genuineness that was irresistible to most.

One evening he was on a big spread in the Osage, interviewing a wealthy rancher for a story. At some point in his host's home, the rancher turned the tables on Allen, earnestly quizzing him about his career and the many stories—and characters—he had written about along the way.

N. Beachey Musselman (1897-1963), editor and manager of the *Shawnee News-Star*, consistent winner of editorial writing awards, member of the Oklahoma State Regents for Higher Education, president of the Oklahoma Press Association (1961).

Dr. Ray Tassin (1926-2011), leader of Central State University's journalism program in 1961, owner, editor, and publisher of *The Konawa Leader*, author of five books and 600 articles, decorated commander of the Naval Reserve, founder of Oklahoma Journalism Hall of Fame.

Vivian E. Vahlberg (1948-), first female president of the National Press Club, assistant Washington Bureau chief for *The Daily Oklahoman* and *Oklahoma City Times*, covering a wide range of national and international stories.

— 1984

Robert B. Allen (1914-1982), reporter for *The Oklahoman* and *Oklahoma City Times*, worked for the *Cushing Daily Citizen* and various Texas papers, managing editor and telegraph editor for the *Norman Transcript*.

Ralph E. Cain, Sr. (1898-1968), community newspaper leader, founder of the *Vici Beacon*, owner of *Yale News*, press secretary for Congressman Victor Wickersham in Washington, news editor for the *Oklahoma Publisher*.

O.B. Campbell (1905-1992), editor and publisher of the *Vinita Daily Journal*, founder of the Eastern Trails Museum, founder of the Craig County Historical Society, served on the Board of Directors of the Oklahoma Historical Society, historical book author.

Hugh C. Hall (1906-1990), worked with the *Henryetta Daily Free-Lance,* served as city reporter, city editor, and Capitol reporter at the *Oklahoma City Times,* served on the Henryetta City Council.

Wesley K. Leatherock (1897-1949), widely known in the Southwest for his work in the American Legion and Rotary, publisher of the *Perry Daily Journal*, founder of the *Clinton Daily News*, owner of other papers in Oklahoma, Texas, and Kansas.

S. George Little (1903-1974), founder, board chairman, and publisher of General Features Corp., worked for *The Daily Oklahoman* and the *Ada Daily News*, publisher of 10 Long Island, New York newspapers, special consultant to the secretary of the treasury in national war bond promotions for World War II.

Clyde Muchmore (1884-1959), publisher of *The Ponca City News* for 40 years, active member in several organizations, treasurer of the Oklahoma Society of Crippled Children.

Stella M. Roberts (1922-1990), first female elected national secretary treasurer of the Wire Service Guild, worked with the *Okemah Leader*, The Associated Press, the Oklahoma City Bureau, and the Capitol Bureau, served as public information director for the Oklahoma Employment Security Commission.

Sidney J. Steen (1908-1992), Oklahoma journalist for more than a half century, worked with the *Arkansas Gazette, Okmulgee Times,* and *Tulsa Tribune,* executive editor for the *Tulsa World.*

— **1985**

Jack Bickham (1930-1997), educator, author of 61 published books, including westerns, mysteries, comedies, and science fiction, professor at the University of Oklahoma School of Journalism, prizewinning writer, editor for a number of Oklahoma newspapers.

Ed Burchfiel (1911-1999), writer, editor, and publisher credited with introducing offset printing to daily newspapers in Oklahoma, worked with the *Tulsa World,* publisher and owner of the *Cordell Beacon.*

Roy Butterbaugh (1898-1971), published the *Cimarron News* of Boise City for 40 years, served as governor of Rotary International District 569, choir director of his church for more than 30 years, published a 144-page history of Cimarron County.

James J. Downing (1914-1981), worked 15 years for United Press International, owner of Ohio newspaper *The Sharon Spectator,* editor and columnist for the *Tulsa Tribune,* editor of the *Bixby Bulletin,* author of four novels.

Charles E. Engleman (1911-2003), editor and publisher of the *Clinton Daily News* for 45 years, named "Benefactor of the Year" by the University of Oklahoma School of Journalism (1978), presented the 1982 Milt Phillips Award for Excellence in newspaper journalism by the Oklahoma Press Association, president of the OU Board of Regents.

Don Ferrell (1929-), state senator, publisher of the *Chandler Lincoln County News,* press secretary to Governor Henry Bellmon, served in the Air Force and Air National Guard, active member and president of the Oklahoma Press Association (1984).

Robert L. Kidd, Sr. (1876-1959), editorial writer, founder of the *Spiro Times,* publisher and owner of the *Poteau News,* wrote the "Down Memory Lane" weekly column for many years, Oklahoma Press Association vice president, honored by the OPA for 50 years of service in newspapering in Oklahoma.

J. Nelson Taylor (1900-1992), worked with the *Tulsa World, The Oklahoman,* and *Oklahoma City Times* for a combined 40 years, covered the Pretty Boy Floyd story in the early 1930s, recognized as the Sigma Delta Chi Newsman of the Year (1971).

 **Howard M. Wilson** (1916-2005), Oklahoma political and legislative reporter, worked for the *New York Civil Service Leader,* the *Tulsa World, The Oklahoman,* and *Oklahoma City Times,* the United Press and the *Oil and Gas Journal,* partner with the Capitol News Bureau in Oklahoma City.

— 1986

 **Glen Bayless** (1916-1989), reporter for the *Oklahoma News* and the United Press, writer and editor for *Newsweek* and *Business Week,* public relations practitioner, worked for the business news department of *The Daily Oklahoman.*

 **Edith Walker Forbes** (1901-1984), publisher of the *Times-Record* in Gotebo, taught in Oklahoma and the Philippines, published weeklies in the 1930s with her husband, Raymond Forbes.

 **Richard L. Jones, Jr.** (1909-1982), president of the *Tulsa Tribune* for 30 years, president of the Southern Newspaper Publishers Association, chairman of the Bureau of Advertising for the American Newspaper Publishers Association, served as director of The Associated Press.

 **Wallace Kidd** (1915-1986), editor and co-publisher of the *Anadarko Daily News,* president of the Oklahoma Press Association (1965), president of the Oklahoma Chapter of the Society of Professional Journalists, Sigma Delta Chi.

 **Edward F. Montgomery** (1918-2009), worked for the *Shelby County Herald* in Missouri, served as bombardier and navigator in World War II, on staff at *The Daily Oklahoman,* the *Oklahoma City Times,* the *Oklahoma Farmer-Stockman,* and the *Norman Transcript,* city editor and Capital Bureau head for *The Oklahoman.*

 **James L. "Jim" Pate** (1932-2011), director, treasurer, vice president, and president of the National Newspaper Association, co-publisher of the *Madill Record* and *The Texhoman,* president of the Oklahoma Press Association (1974) and the Oklahoma Newspaper Foundation.

 **Herbert J. Pate** (1903-1990), carrier boy for the *Hobart Daily Republican,* city editor of the *Miami Tribune* (Florida), owner of the *Madill Record* and various other papers, established KMAD Radio in Madill, served as president of the Oklahoma Press Association (1950).

 **James T. Young** (1923-2005), reported on presidential visits to Oklahoma from Dwight D. Eisenhower to Ronald Reagan, worked with *The Oklahoman* and *Oklahoma City Times* for 35 years, served in the Air Force in World War II, worked with the *Cleveland County Times, Edinburg Daily Review, Henryetta Dally Free-Lance,* and the Oklahoma Publishing Company.

James R. Bellatti (1927-2016), general manager of KSPI and KSPI-FM for 10 years, publisher of the *Stillwater News Press*, president of the Oklahoma Broadcasters Association, president of the Oklahoma Press Association (1981), first Oklahoman to head the World Alliance of the YMCA.

Bill F. Bentley (1924-1997), editor and publisher of *The Lawton Constitution* and *Morning Press*, Purple Heart recipient from World War II, member of several press organizations, worked with the Lawton Publishing Company.

Carter Bradley (1919-2008), worked with United Press International, served on the staff of the U.S. Senate Committee on Aeronautical and Space Sciences, administrative assistant to Senator. A.S. "Mike" Monroney, executive director of the Higher Education Alumni Council of Oklahoma, partner in the Oklahoma Press Association Capitol News Bureau.

Richard Franklin "Dick" Dudley (1905-1978), publisher of the *Hollis Daily News* for 35 years, civic and church leader; promoted business, industry, and agriculture in his community with his column, "Across the Desk."

Ruth Robinson Greenup (1912-1984), traveled to South America in 1940 to work for Reuters and edit papers in Brazil and Argentina, worked with her husband, Leonard Greenup, in writing *Revolution Before Breakfast: Argentina 1941-1946.*

Richard R. Hefton (1930-), president, editor, and publisher of Oklahoma County Newspapers Incorporated, executive member of the *McAlester News Capital* and *The Journal Record*, president of the Oklahoma Press Association (1975) and Suburban Associated Newspapers, Inc., promoted by President Ronald Reagan to brigadier general in the Air Force.

Ennis C. "Tex" Helm (1903-1982), set a world record by photographing Carlsbad Caverns National Park with 2,400 flashbulbs, photographer on *The Oklahoman* and *Oklahoma City Times*, author of *Patience*, a book focusing on his life in Oklahoma.

Joe Howell (1910-1998), worked with the *Tulsa Tribune* as a carrier boy, reporter, and expert on politics and government, covered seven full terms of the Oklahoma Legislature, helped cover the election or administration of every governor since 1937.

Irvin Hurst (1904-1995), political and government writer, reporter, and city editor for *The Oklahoman* and *Times*, insurance company executive, author of 46th Star, which gives an account of early statehood days and the moving of the capital to Oklahoma City.

George W. Cornell (1921-1994), religion writer for The Associated Press, reporter for *The Daily Oklahoman*, served in the Army, winner of many journalistic excellence awards for his books, articles, and weekly columns.

Lola Hall (1933-), worked for KWTV in Oklahoma City as a reporter, and as the "Channel 9 Weather Girl," and for a number of other television and radio stations in Oklahoma City, and for NBC in New York City.

Charles Nedwin "Ned" Hockman (1921-2009), pioneer of photojournalism in Oklahoma, the U.S. Air Corps, and the U.S. Air Force, recipient of the John A. Sprague Memorial Award (1985).

John A. Jameson (1905-1985), worked with The Associated Press in Tulsa, Oklahoma City, Kansas City, and New York City, served as AP bureau chief in Indianapolis and Denver, published the *Englewood Herald* in Colorado, served as president of the Colorado Press Association.

Wayne Mackey (1921-1987), worked with *The Daily Oklahoman, Oklahoma City Times, Austin American Statesman, San Antonio Evening News,* and *Tonkawa News*, Navy veteran, president of the Oklahoma Chapter of the Society of Professional Journalists.

Alfred W. "Al" McLaughlin (1921-2013), chief photographer for the Oklahoma Publishing Company, served in the U.S. Air Force during World War II, consultant at *The Oklahoman*, recipient of the National Women's Page Photographer of the Year title (1966) and the National Picture Layout Award given by the JCPenney Company (1968).

Gareth B. Muchmore (1913-1983), covered World War II for The Associated Press, head of AP's financial news department in New York, managing editor and co-publisher of *The Ponca City News*, Radio Station WBBZ partner, editor of the *Duncan Banner*.

Montez Tjaden (1913-1993), management team member in starting KWTV in Oklahoma City and KRMG in Tulsa, served in theater, radio, television, newspaper, public relations, and the U.S. Navy, national president of Women in Radio and Television.

Jerry L. Witcher (1932-2006), United Press International member, Oklahoma bureau manager, state editor, reporter, and editor for the *Altus Times-Democrat*, member of the Oklahoma City Gridiron Club.

Freda Ameringer (1892-1988), started the Leader Press Incorporated, the *Oklahoma City Advertiser*, and the *Daily Law Journal Record*, now *The Journal Record*, with her father, co-founded the Oklahoma City Urban League and the Pilot Club.

Byron Vest Boone (1908-1988), legal, civic, and community affairs leader in Tulsa, lawyer, general counsel to the *Tulsa World*, publisher of the *Tulsa World* for almost 30 years.

Chuck Ervin (1937-2011), political and governmental writer, worked with the *McAlester News-Capital*, bureau chief of the *Tulsa World* state capitol bureau, winner of several writing awards, including one from Sigma Delta Chi for coverage of the McAlester prison riot.

Channing E. Guffey (1924-2007), established *Guffey's Journal*, editor and writer for *The Daily Oklahoman*, worked with the *Woodward Daily Press*, *Watonga Republican*, and the *Daily Globe* in Dodge City, Kansas.

Edith Kinney Gaylord (1916-2001), worked for *The Oklahoman* and *Oklahoma City Times*, worked as a Washington Bureau reporter for the Associated Press, president of the Women's National Press Club, secretary and director of the Oklahoma Publishing Company, founder of the Ethics and Excellence in Journalism Foundation.

Joe White McBride, Jr. (1929-), general manager and publisher of the award-winning *Anadarko Daily News*, president of the Oklahoma Press Association (1987), the Oklahoma City Press Club, the Oklahoma Lung Association, the Anadarko Chamber of Commerce, and the UPI Editors of Oklahoma.

Roy P. Stewart (1905-1989), city editor, Washington Bureau chief, columnist, and editorial writer for *The Daily Oklahoman*, military officer, historian, author of several books, writer for national publications.

Richard David Story (1952-), worked with *Reader's Digest* as a fact checker, senior editor for *New York Magazine*, entertainment reporter for *USA Today*, editor of *Destinations*, worked with *Esquire, Metropolitan Home, Travel & Leisure, Departures,* and *American Way*.

Tom Yarbrough (1910-1975), reporter, war correspondent, and feature writer for 44 years, worked with the *Oklahoma City Times* and The Associated Press, head of the AP office in St. Louis, Missouri, worked with the *St. Louis Post-Dispatch*.

THE 1990s
authors, a cartoonist, and the founding father of Oklahoma journalism

Journalists who became authors began to populate the Hall of Fame more in the 1990s.

Joseph H. "Joe" Carter, Sr. went from a United Press International reporter to writing books and portraying Will Rogers, who entered the Hall of Fame 21 years before Carter's induction in 1992. Then there was famed mystery writer Tony Hillerman, who was inducted in 1993. Eric Allen, inducted in 1994, was an author, screenwriter, and onetime president of the Western Writers of America. Stan Hoig, inducted the same year, was noted for his western history books. Reba Collins, also noted for her books about and knowledge of Will Rogers, was inducted in 1998.

Photographers, Capitol Bureau correspondents, news anchors, columnists, community journalists, publishers, and one editorial cartoonist, Jim Lange, also were prominent additions.

Lange's biography noted that "He has used his enormous storehouse of energy and talent for the betterment of his community, state, and nation, as well as his profession."

Despite the Oklahoma City bombing that shocked the world in 1995, the Hall of Fame continued its tradition of annual inductions. W.P. "Bill" Atkinson, Donovan Banzett, James W. Bradshaw, Klina E. Casady, Paul English, Marlan Dee Nelson, Max J. Nichols, Omer F. Schnoebelen, and Milo W. Watson became members that year.

And, in 1998, the Hall of Fame inducted its first-born member, considered the "founding father of Oklahoma Journalism." The photo of William P. Ross, who was born in 1820 and died in 1891, shows him sitting in a chair staring intently at the camera. His hair and beard are completely white, a small part in the back seemingly fluff and out of place.

Ross was a Cherokee Nation chief and founding editor of the "first newspaper in what is now Oklahoma, the *Cherokee Advocate*. He also edited the *Indian Journal* at Eufaula, the oldest newspaper in Oklahoma, the *Indian Chieftain,* and the *Indian Arrow*."

One year after Ross, Dennie Hall accepted his selection into the Hall of Fame. It came two years after he retired as Hall of Fame director.

Framed! Jim Mayo with his son, Jeff Mayo. Date unknown.

A son's tribute to dad, Jim Lange, by Robert Lange.

Ken Neal (left) talks with artist Brummett Echohawk about some of his experiences during World War II. One of Brummett's pieces of art hangs on the wall behind him. Photographer: Joe Iverson. Courtesy of the *Tulsa World*.

Alex Adwan Media Icon award collage. Courtesy of the *Tulsa World*.

Ken Neal. Courtesy of the *Tulsa World*.

Colonial Delegates to the U.S. Constitutional Convention were portrayed Friday by students at Coronado Heights Elementary School. May 4, 1973, *The Daily Oklahoman,* Jim Argo photo. Courtesy of the Oklahoma Historical Society.

Arthur B. Ramsey, pioneer Oklahoma newsreel cameraman. Date unknown.

Portraits of former Gov. and Mrs. Henry S. Johnston are propped among their possessions, which were auctioned to the highest bidders in Perry on Saturday. June 2, 1980, *Oklahoma City Times*. Jim Argo photo. Courtesy of the Oklahoma Historical Society.

Biding the time this morning until her fellow felines arrive, Lisa the lion waits impatiently for other animals in the Shrine Circus. A delay in Tulsa will not affect tonight's opening of a four-day appearance at the State Fair Arena. March 25, 1981. *The Daily Oklahoman*. Jim Argo photo. Courtesy of the Oklahoma Historical Society.

Mary Jo Nelson (center) and former OU football coach Bud Wilkinson (left). November 3, 1964. Photo by Bob Heaton. Copyright, 1964, Oklahoma Publishing Co.

Left to right: *The Oklahoman* and Hall of Fame reporters Mick Hinton, Michael McNutt, John Greiner, and Jon Denton gather for Greiner's birthday celebration in Oklahoma City.

JOHN GREINER

Henry Bellmon and me

By John Greiner, 1993 Inductee

When Henry Bellmon left the U.S. Senate, he was appointed by Governor George Nigh to head the Department of Human Services, also known as the Welfare Department.

Bellmon wasted no time in developing a reorganization plan for the massive agency. When he was ready to present the plan to the agency's board of directors, he did so in the agency's small board room. He would not release the plan at that time to the news media but made them wait until the meeting ended.

At a break, I went straight to Bellmon to explain why we reporters should have a copy of the report during the meeting. I argued it would make it easier for us to get things right.

"Do you want to run this agency?" growled Bellmon, sounding like the Marine he was.

Associated Press reporter Ron Jenkins grinned. After the meeting we got the report, as promised.

Bellmon came to me, Jenkins, and other reporters. He told us if he had released the report to reporters, Harry Culver of United Press International and Jim Young of the *Oklahoma City Times* would have gone back to the press room and filed their stories.

"I would have spent the rest of the afternoon answering phone calls [of other reporters]," Bellmon said.

Reporters gather to interview Governor David Walters in the Governor's Conference Room.

Hall of Famers John Greiner (left), Paul English, and Mick Hinton pose for a picture outside the state capitol building in the 90s. Photo by Jim Argo.

Governor Henry Bellmon and John Greiner, right.

Ron Jenkins (left), AP State Capitol Bureau Chief and *The Oklahoman's* John Greiner in the state House of Representatives covering the dedication of a portrait of Ada Lois Sipuel Fisher. June 19, 2007.

JAMES R. "JIM" CAMPBELL
a byline with ten-million words of integrity

By Joseph H. Carter, Sr., 1992 Inductee

For you who have seen the MSNBC interviews from our nation's Capitol, standing behind that on-camera politician is a fellow in bronze: that's the real Will Rogers, keeping his eyes on Congress.

Equally solid is James R. Campbell in capturing the essence of Oklahoma's favorite son. Campbell was a great writer, pundit, and Oklahoma newsman who surely equaled Will Rogers' integrity, good humor, and search for truth.

When Wiley Post slammed his plane into the sea near Point Barrow, Alaska, Campbell was only three years old. What was left of the life, writings, words, and wisdom of Will Rogers were dissolved into the ages.

I propose that much of that evasive, folksy, truth-telling talent seems to have settled and grown on Campbell.

From United Press International bureaus of America and the press room at the Oklahoma Capitol, we have been blessed with seeing the Will Rogers-like persona of James Campbell. Later, when he played "Mr. Voter" in the Oklahoma City Gridiron, it became even more obvious.

Lucky for me, when I was hired by United Press International in 1959, Campbell was already aboard as a wire service correspondent at the Oklahoma City bureau, atop the Skirvin Tower. He became my mentor, editor, collaborator, and friend.

A year earlier, Campbell had graduated from a $70-per-week reporting job at the *Bartlesville Examiner Enterprise* to $80-per-week as a UPI correspondent. I was in Campbell's vortex from the *Sapulpa Herald*. Both Army veterans. Same salaries. Same new challenges of tough deadline writing, unbiased but verified reporting to be tested by many newspaper editors and TV journalists.

Biographers calculate that Will Rogers published some two million words. I calculate that with over 30 years at United Press International, Jim Campbell wrote many more—more than 10 million words. Most of those words Campbell wrote were carefully selected. Broadcasters and editors demand truth, clarity, and copy written brightly but sprightly. Also, no misspelled words for print media.

For Campbell, few readers and newscast listeners knew at the time about the rigorous tests faced by each of those millions of words written and sent over the wires of UPI under the "James R. Campbell" byline.

The mandate was: get it first, but first get it right. As Campbell and I learned back in the 1950s, UPI's slogan was "Deadline Every Minute." It meant that somewhere a newspaper was going to press or a newscast was about to begin. The demand was for the delivery of the latest news "right now" but to first get it "right." And, perfect spelling. All of the writing and reporting by Campbell was under that pressure for more than 30 years. He never flinched.

In this new electronic age, unverified, unedited Facebook posts and tweets have been unleashed onto the vulnerable minds of humanity. In contrast, Campbell rose in a world of higher education, of fine training, of high-pressure writing, of fact-checking editors, and from tested and rigorous standards of established professional journalism.

Something Will Rogers said years ago has become appropriate today: "It may be years before there is much 'new' news. It's going to take a new generation of people to make 'new' news."

Hopefully, a new generation of journalists, with their tough editors and demanding readers and listeners, will draw on the life and literacy and tough legacy of great reporting by James R. Campbell.

Working journalists, students of the trade, and historians can be advised that the James R. Campbell byline meant unbiased, non-partisan, honest, well-written, and always reliable news reporting. Never "fake news."

Let us rekindle and keep the "Campbell Standard" and legacy alive—forever.

Photograph used for a story in *The Daily Oklahoman* newspaper. "Gridiron Club President Jim Campbell, left, shows the program to Gov. Nigh." Doug Hoke, February 17, 1979. Courtesy of the Oklahoma Historical Society.

Jim Campbell (right) enjoys a discussion between fellow colleagues Frosty Troy (left) and John Greiner.

This essay was adapted from the eulogy that Joseph H. Carter, Sr. delivered at the funeral of Jim Campbell on December 9, 2018. Carter wore a Will Rogers costume in delivering the eulogy. Campbell's daughter, Jenifer Reynolds, has been a member since 2005.

1995: THE OKLAHOMA CITY BOMBING
that exact moment that changed Hall of Famers' lives forever

By Joe Hight, 2013 Inductee

That exact moment.

Many members of the Oklahoma Journalism Hall of Fame probably remember when they heard or felt the blast that changed so many lives on April 19, 1995.

I know I do. At work that morning, I felt the blast's impact hit the side of *The Oklahoman's* building seven miles to the north and shake it like a stalk in an Oklahoma wheat field. I later visited the bombing site and toured the area around it. I saw the media city that had developed with the throngs of journalists who traveled to Oklahoma City to cover the tragedy that affected the world.

That exact moment.

Kari Watkins, the Oklahoma City National Memorial & Museum Executive Director, understands the important role that local journalists played at that point in time and afterward. It's commemorated as part of the permanent display in the museum today.

"I think local journalists set a standard for the national media to follow," Watkins told me. "It was incredibly personal to them."

Those standards included developing models for future coverage, including vignettes about the victims' lives, information on how the community could help and how the victims could get help, stories about acts of kindness in the community, and a balance of coverage in telling the complete story with the victims' and community's perspective, not just ones about the perpetrators who committed the terrorist act.

"Print, radio, and television all set standards for all national and local media to follow. They changed the perspective of how to tell stories. They were our neighbors, our brothers and sisters … We began to tell the story that they, the victims, were like us," Watkins said.

"Other media should use their example as a resource. Local journalists did a great job in telling the story. What we witnessed was devastating. Our hearts were torn apart by the act of terrorism in downtown Oklahoma City. I think it was the hardest story to cover, but they did with knowledge and insight."

That exact moment.

It fueled researchers and others to study journalists' coverage of their communities in the aftermath of tragedy. It fueled my interest in trauma and journalism that continues to this day. I was involved in the founding of the international Dart Center for Journalism and Trauma, which is dedicated to sensitive coverage of victims and tragedy. It led me to recognize the vital role the media play in the aftermath of these tragedies. We'll always remember that exact moment which changed our lives, but we never want it to happen again to our community.

To any community. To any person.

Joe Hight coordinated the national "Institute on Coverage of Disasters and Tragedies: Writing and Editing Better Stories about Victims" after suggesting The Oklahoman *use the $10,000 it won from the Dart Award for Excellence in Coverage of Violence. More than 200 people attended the workshop on April 5, 1997, at the University of Central Oklahoma.*

Joe Hight runs a planning meeting at *The Oklahoman* in the aftermath of the bombing. Also pictured are reporter Tony Thornton and news editor Ed Sargent, who shows the stress of the coverage. Photo courtesy of the Oklahoma City National Memorial & Museum.

DAVID PAGE
cup of coffee may have saved him
By Ralph Schaefer, 2107 Inductee

A cup of coffee probably saved David Page from serious injury when his editor's office inside *The Journal Record* was extensively damaged on April 19, 1995.

The target was the Alfred P. Murrah Federal Building, but surrounding buildings were badly damaged, and many were later destroyed.

Page, the newspaper's managing editor, had gone to work at 7:30 a.m. The sun was shining brightly at about 9:00 a.m. when he stepped away from his desk on the building's first floor that faced the Murrah building for that cup of coffee—one he never got to drink.

"I could see the federal building, and if I had seen the truck, I would not have thought anything about it," said Page, who was inducted into the Hall of Fame in 2011. "Everyone was going about their business."

Page was returning to his office when the bomb exploded, and he was covered with glass from *The Journal Record* windows that had been blown inward.

"I checked the composition room, then walked outside a north entrance to the nearby parking garage," he said.

A garage attendant saw Page was bleeding, he provided a bandage and a clean garage rag for his only apparent wound. He later would require 30 stitches for other injuries.

Initially, Page thought the explosion occurred inside *The Journal Record* building. After he received help at the parking garage, he walked to the south side of the newspaper building and saw the Murrah Building. Injured people were being taken to area hospitals. Page was treated at a local hospital. Three doctors stitched up his wounds and a priest called June, his wife, to take him home.

"The doctors wanted to get to me and others less seriously injured, so they could be ready for other casualties," he said.

When daughter Mary and son Daniel arrived from school, the family went shopping for Page. His glasses had been lost in the explosion and his clothes had been removed at the hospital, so he could be checked for any glass that might be in his body.

"I went home in a hospital gown," he recalled.

Telephone calls came that evening from reporters checking on Page, as well as media and The Associated Press wanting to talk to him for stories. Page would be on CNN and *Dateline*.

Despite the loss of their offices and printing capabilities, *The Journal Record* staff met at Remington Park on April 20 to look at publishing the next issue.

The access to computers was the greatest obstacle.

A University of Central Oklahoma graduate and staff member noted the public relations department had computers that might be available.

The university's facilities were available, and a two-page broadsheet was published with staff members writing about their experiences. That was expanded to four pages and more during the upcoming weeks.

The Edmond Sun printed *The Journal Record's* first newspaper after the bombing.

Page and staff writer Kirby Davis returned to the damaged Journal Record Building on April 20, the day after the bombing, to retrieve documents and personal items, but were chased out by FBI agents searching for evidence. Page and Davis returned about a week later to recover various items.

Today, part of *The Journal Record's* building houses the Oklahoma City National Memorial & Museum. The wreckage of Page's office where he would have returned with that cup of coffee is preserved as part of the exhibits.

Statistics tabulated by the Oklahoma City Bombing report—courtesy of the Tinker Historians office—noted that while estimated damage would exceed $650 million, the exact cost could never be tabulated. It was estimated that 168 people died that day. At least 600 were hospitalized; 30 children were orphaned; 219 children lost one parent; more than 300 buildings were damaged or destroyed; 462 people were left homeless; and 2,000 vehicles were demolished.

LINDEL HUTSON
story behind Pulitzer Prize photo
By Lindel Hutson, 2008 Inductee

It is three hours after a bomb ripped open the Alfred P. Murrah Federal Building, and The Associated Press bureau in Oklahoma City is in a frenzy.

Our phones ring nonstop. Reporters call in dictation. Photographers hustle to transmit images. Every executive in New York wants me. There's an old saying in the AP: there's a deadline every minute, and the clock was ticking loudly that sunny but bleak morning of April 19, 1995. We are center stage worldwide.

Into this mania steps a fair-haired, bespectacled young man wearing a confused look. He walks up to the receptionist and asks if we want to buy photos from downtown. She directs him to the photo area, where I stand behind photographer David Longstreath. The initial reaction is, what can this young guy whose hobby is photography possibly have to forward our coverage of the nation's biggest story? After all, we're the pros. Who is he?

Charles Porter IV had gone through the trouble to have his film processed and I decided to look at his prints rather than politely ask him to leave. He had a look of sincerity about him, and I didn't want to be rude even in the midst of chaos.

I flipped through a half-dozen pictures that were not wire worth.

Then the next photo stunned me.

Porter's photo showed a fireman cradling a bloodied baby. It was one of the most heart-wrenching photos I had ever seen. To this day it is hard for me to look at.

It would become the iconic image of the Oklahoma City bombing. Porter had two photos that I purchased after some brief negotiations. The baby was tiny Baylee Almon. She would have turned one year old the next day. She died shortly after the photo was taken, but we did not know that at the time.

Holding her was firefighter Chris Fields. In one of the photos—which did not get much use—Fields is being handed the baby by a police officer who had pulled her from the rubble.

When transmitted, the photo of Fields holding Baylee took on a life of its own. It was on the front page of nearly every newspaper around the world. It was on the cover of *Newsweek* Magazine.

Porter, the mild-mannered bank teller who had only recently graduated from the University of Central Oklahoma, became an instant celebrity. His photo was named photo of the year by the British press photographers and Porter and his wife were flown to London for the award. For AP, it won the 1996 Pulitzer Prize for spot news photography.

His was the classic case of being in the right place at the right time and getting the right advice. After he snapped the pictures, he took the film to Walmart for processing. There, the women who worked the film became the first to see the pictures and started crying.

Unsure what to do with the photos, Porter called a friend from UCO who suggested he contact Woody Gaddis. Gaddis built the photography program at UCO and was inducted into the Hall of Fame in 2005.

Gaddis thought the photos needed the widest distribution possible, and suggested Porter go to AP.

MILO WATSON
the biggest story on his biggest day
By Ed Kelley 2003 Inductee

The day in 1995 Milo Watson received the biggest honor of his career was the same day he missed the biggest story of his career.

'Tis true. I know, because I was the messenger who delivered the word to him that the most notorious criminal in Oklahoma history was sitting in jail in Perry, where Watson was publisher, while Watson was being feted 45 miles away by the Oklahoma Journalism Hall of Fame.

The back story:

My start in newspapering came thanks to Watson, who let me write sports stories for the *Perry Daily Journal* while in high school. He gave me oodles of space and even paid me a little something for my efforts. Later he was kind enough to write a letter on my behalf to the journalism school at the University of Oklahoma. Forever I have been indebted for his interest in me.

So, years later, when word came that he was named to the Hall of Fame's class of 1995, I wanted to repay my debt in a small way.

Back then the hall's induction came at an afternoon ceremony and reception. So, I organized a luncheon on April 21 at a nice restaurant on Edmond's east side, where I met him, his two daughters, his wife, June, and Bob Lee, who was inducted one year later in 1996. Lee was a colleague of mine at *The Oklahoman* and, more importantly, was a charter member of the Milo Watson Fan Club. That's because Lee's dad, Ed, employed a young Watson at the Lee family newspaper in Buffalo, in Harper County. And a young Bobby Lee looked up to Watson the rest of his life.

When lunch was finished, everyone went their separate ways to the University of Central Oklahoma campus for the induction. But first I called the office, as this was the busiest week of my career. So happened that the Murrah building was bombed two days earlier, on April 19. And as managing editor, I owned the coverage. I made the call just to check in, to see if anything was new.

"Well, you'll never guess what happened," said the secretary on the other end of the line. The gist: a man suspected of the bombing, later identified as Timothy McVeigh, was being held in the Noble County Jail in Perry, my hometown.

I gunned the engine and got to UCO ahead of Watson and his girls.

I wanted to be the one to give him the news, right there in the parking lot. On a sunny spring afternoon, I met the now elderly man who gave me my start as he strode toward me. "You're not going to believe this," is how I started.

His knees, no kidding, buckled.

Fortunately he didn't fall.

Fortunately he had trained his staff to proceed without him. Because in that Friday afternoon paper was a short story at the top of the front page—not brimming with details, because there weren't many at the time. But a story, nevertheless.

Fortunately the folks in Perry continued to get another couple of years of his leadership before ill health forced him down. All told he spent nearly 55 years at the *Journal*, all but the first six as publisher.

As someone who was weaned on his newspaper, I will venture this:

Milo Watson, *Perry Daily Journal* publisher, pictured surrounded by his work in his office. He was the 1967 Oklahoma Press Association president. Photo by Jim Argo. Date unknown. Courtesy of the Oklahoma Historical Society.

that one day in 1995, when he missed out on the biggest story in town since the Land Run, doesn't begin to overshadow the thousands of great days that Watson was at the helm, firmly guiding the community he informed. And occasionally cajoled.

And loved, most of all.

Milo Watson died at 83 years old, after his induction in 1998. His wife, Anne, preceded him in death in 1987. According to a story in The Oklahoman, he was survived by "two daughters and sons-in-law, Carolyn and Richard Adkins, Fort Gibson, and John and Mary Lee Streller, Newalla; five grandchildren and 11 great-grandchildren."

LINDA CAVANAUGH
'The Hanoi Hilton' and the day of tragedy in my own hometown
By Linda Cavanaugh, 1998 Inductee

From the air, it was a beautiful sight. Our plane had begun the descent to land in Vietnam, and I marveled at the number of small blue lakes that dotted the countryside. Former Vietnam prisoner of war and Navy pilot Dan Glenn—who hadn't seen the country since his release decades earlier—took a look and said matter-of-factly, "Those are rain-filled bomb craters."

It was the beginning of a trip that would take him back to a time when he and other U.S. military prisoners of war were held in conditions so harsh and inhumane that atrocities were a way of life.

"All the movies tell you when the pain gets too bad, you pass out," he said. "You don't pass out."

We didn't know it at the time, but our April 1995 trip back to Vietnam would make history.

It was a journey months in the making.

I had contacted Glenn at his home in Norman, Oklahoma, to ask if he would consider returning to Vietnam.

I explained that I was producing a documentary to mark the twenty-fifth anniversary of the Fall of Saigon and the end of the war in Vietnam. The controversial war had captured headlines during my high school and college years—and took the lives of many of those still smiling from the pages of my yearbooks.

At first, he declined.

But then, several weeks later, Glenn called me to say he'd changed his mind. He was willing to go back.

After weeks of planning, Glenn, photographer Tony Stizza, and I arrived in Vietnam to begin a trip that would take us into the notorious Cu Chi tunnels—the underground lair where Viet Cong lay in wait for U.S. infantry. After several requests, we were able to talk with a former Viet Cong general, who, with his family, lived in a hut on the outskirts of the jungle.

But our ultimate goal was to return to the infamous "Hanoi Hilton," the prison where Glenn was taken in 1966 as a 26-year-old Navy pilot, shot down and captured four days before Christmas.

"I was worried about surviving the day," Glenn said.

He had no way of knowing that one day would turn into a six-year nightmare of incarceration.

Yet, he wanted to return.

Our request for entry into the abandoned prison was not the first to be made by journalists. All had been declined. But we persisted. We stood outside of the locked gate and waited. For eight hours, we waited.

Finally, a man arrived with a large metal key, walked up to the gate and opened it.

We became the first journalists to enter the notorious prison where hundreds of American POWs had been interrogated and tortured.

When the gate swung open, Glenn didn't hesitate. He headed directly to the room where he was first taken and introduced to "The Rabbit," a man known for his especially cruel torture techniques. Glenn remembered a meat hook that hung from the ceiling.

After a few minutes, he began to cry. I suggested that we step outside for fresh air. He hesitated, looked at me, and said something I'll never forget.

"I'm crying because I'm remembering the incredible love POWs had for each other in this place."

My family and friends worried about our safety in Vietnam. But, one night as our trip was nearing its end in Hanoi, I awakened to hear a voice on the hotel television frantically describing a scene of horrible destruction. The voice sounded oddly familiar. It was one of our Channel 4 reporters.

I got out of bed and walked toward the screen to see smoke pouring from a building whose front was torn away. Papers were still floating down from the top stories. First responders were rushing into the debris of a downtown Oklahoma City building.

It was April 19, 1995.

Linda Cavanaugh has been called "Oklahoma's First Lady of Television News." Her journalism career spanned more than four decades. Linda began her career in newspapers before working in New York as a magazine writer. She returned to Oklahoma City to begin her broadcasting career.

Hall of Famers Linda Cavanaugh and Tony Stizza shoot footage in the countryside near Hanoi, Vietnam. April 1995.

This is the Pulitzer Prize-winning photo of Oklahoma City firefighter Chris Fields carrying 1-year-old Baylee Almon after the Oklahoma City bombing on April 19, 1995. The photo has become the iconic image of the bombing. Charles Porter IV/ZUMAPRESS.com

BILLIE RODELY

unspeakable horror of that day

By Billie Rodely, 2003 Inductee

It wasn't writer's block or a simple loss for words. That day 25 years ago the only word I could conjure was "unspeakable." A reporter for radio is to paint word pictures for listeners, but I simply couldn't bring myself to turn on the tape recorder and speak.

Countless articles and books have chronicled the atrocity of the Oklahoma City bombing on April 19, 1995. So many that, over the years, I just let others tell the story. I certainly was not a good or even adequate professional journalist that day.

The sights, smells, sounds, and palpable fear and angst in the air were too overwhelming for me to describe. I failed at first to do my job as I arrived at Fifth Street and Robinson Avenue before the area had been cordoned off and reporters and others were kept at bay.

So, I saw body parts hanging from what we now know as the "Survivor Tree." Literally, a lady's breast still cupped in a lacy white brassiere hanging there.

Unspeakable.

Later, when moved north a block by police, a firefighter passed by me. He had a tow-headed baby cradled in his arms. The right side of the child's head was covered in blood.

Unspeakable.

It was days later that moment in time would become the iconic photograph of little Baylee Almon.

Eventually, the radio reporter emerged to provide action reports and sanitized descriptions of the horrific scene that day. But, to this day, the images remain in my heart and in my head.

Unspeakable.

Smoke pours from the Alfred P. Murrah Federal Building after the bombing. April 19, 1995. *The Daily Oklahoman*. By Jim Argo. Photo courtesy of the Oklahoma Historical Society.

THE REMAINDER OF THE 1990s
William P. Ross: the 'founding father of Oklahoma journalism'
By Emily Siddiqui, Student Editor

William Potter Ross left a legacy of loyalty and service for his country and his people. As the first newspaper editor in Indian Territory, he would come to be known as the "founding father of Oklahoma journalism."

Ross was born in 1820 near Chattanooga, Tennessee, to John G. Ross, from Scotland, and Eliza Ross, a Cherokee. His uncle, Chief John Ross, paid for him to attend high school and the College of New Jersey, now Princeton University, from which he graduated with honors in 1842. Ross returned to find that his home had moved to Indian Territory, due to the Treaty of New Echota. His aunt had perished on the Trail of Tears. That fall, he taught Indian schoolchildren at Fourteen-Mile Creek, near what is now Hulbert, Oklahoma.

The following year, Ross was elected senate clerk for the Cherokee National Council, where he drafted laws and wrote state papers, and helped to construct the Cherokee Constitution.

The Council soon named him editor of the new *Cherokee Advocate,* the first newspaper in Indian Territory. The mission of the *Advocate* was "to inform and encourage the Cherokees in agriculture, education and religion; and to enlighten the world with correct Indian news."

Four years later, Ross resigned his position as editor to go to Washington. He married Mary Jane Ross, his first cousin, in 1846. He then worked as a merchant and lawyer, and represented the Tahlequah District as senator.

As a bilingual, Ross excelled in his professions. "His written arguments are eloquent specimens of the Indian master of English composition," his wife wrote. His work is among the best in Native American literature, although much of his did advocate slavery. His uncle Chief John Ross owned 100 slaves himself.

In 1860, he worked as a secretary for another uncle, Lewis Ross, who was treasurer of the Cherokee Nation.

Initially, Ross sought to remain neutral in the Civil War; but, like the country, the tribe was split. He fought for the South as a lieutenant colonel in John Drew's First Cherokee Mounted Rifles.

Ross was temporarily captured by the North, and rival Indians burned his store. At the war's end, he was a delegate to the peace conference at Fort Smith, Arkansas.

William P. Ross replaced his uncle John Ross as principal chief after John died in 1866. In this position he amended the Cherokee Constitution and helped construct an agreement that would permit Cherokee citizenship for Delaware Indians. Much of his time was spent trying to amend Cherokee relations shattered by the Civil War. Later, when Lewis Downing died while in office, Ross also served the rest of Downing's term as principal chief.

Portrait of William Potter Ross. Original housed in the Archives & Manuscripts Division of the Oklahoma Historical Society.

Ross later worked as editor for the *Indian Journal*, the *Indian Chieftain,* and the *Indian Arrow*. He also served as a Cherokee senator for the Illinois District, on the board of education, and on the court of citizen claims.

Upon his death in 1891, the family of William Potter Ross received numerous letters of condolence, many of which expressed deep reverence for his legacy. As one friend wrote: "All felt that the noblest man in the Cherokee Nation had fallen." Ross is buried at the Fort Gibson Citizens Cemetery in eastern Oklahoma.

Ross was inducted into the Oklahoma Journalism Hall of Fame in 1998, 107 years after his death.

Sources for this story include the Oklahoma Historical Society, Princeton Historical page, and Cherokee Chief history.

BOB BARRY AND BOB BARRY, JR.
the father-son bond
By Linda Cavanaugh, 1998 Inductee

It was a daily ritual in our newsroom. A special moment between father and son.

Every time Bob Barry, Jr. (BBJ) came in for his shift, he'd make his way over to his legendary sportscasting dad and give him a big, messy kiss on the cheek.

They'd both laugh, hug, and then move on to do what they did best: reporting sports in such a way that they endeared themselves to sports and non-sports fans alike.

The senior Bob Barry's career got a jump start after he fell out of a second story window.

Literally.

The childhood accident required weeks of bedrest. Bob used that time listening to play-by-play calls on the radio and mimicking the rapid-fire delivery of the announcers.

It served him well.

Decades later, when famed University of Oklahoma Football Coach Bud Wilkinson was looking for a new sportscaster to be the voice of the Sooners, he handpicked Bob Barry.

It was a milestone in a career that set the standard for those who followed.

At various times during his five decades in sports, Bob served as the play-by-play announcer for both the University of Oklahoma and Oklahoma State University. Perhaps it's a testament to his fairness and professional demeanor that fans from both rival schools considered him a friend.

Bob was always looking for new ways to entertain viewers while still giving them credible sports information.

That's how our weekly "Football Predictions" segment got started. Bob thought it would be fun if we'd pick the college football teams we believed would win that weekend's games. Bob took it seriously. He talked about the logic behind his choice and went into detail about the game.

I had no clue what I was doing—which is why he asked me to join him.

And yet, I'd consistently win. Blind luck. He said it made it tough to face his golf buddies.

Things didn't always go as planned when we did the predictions.

One week, Bob had the folks at the Oklahoma City Zoo bring out a baby gorilla. The premise was that even a monkey, or gorilla, could predict winners better than Bob. The predictions were going fine until suddenly the gorilla bit Bob's thumb. The Zoo handler rushed up and said, "Has to have a tetanus shot now."

I turned to Bob and said, "Are you current on your tetanus shot?"

Before Bob could answer, the handler grabbed the gorilla and said, "Not Bob! The gorilla!"

Bob lost that week.

Like his dad, BBJ was a guy who loved sports and worked hard every day to get it right.

But BBJ didn't try to copy his dad's style. He had his own. Full of energy and fast-moving.

He'd be out covering an event, rush back to the station, throw on a suit jacket and tie, sit down in the studio, and anchor the sports. What viewers couldn't see because of the anchor desk were the shorts and athletic shoes he didn't bother to change. He knew he'd be heading out to cover the next event as soon as the newscast ended.

BBJ never lacked enthusiasm or the desire to capture the viewer's attention, which may explain what happened that one April Fool's Day in 1982.

BBJ was anchoring the noon news. It was his first year at the station. Just before the commercial break, he announced that then University of Oklahoma Coach Barry Switzer had resigned immediately to become the offensive coordinator for the Dallas Cowboys.

At the same time, the producer was yelling in BBJ's ear piece that he was out of time. So, BBJ tossed to the commercial break without saying "April Fools."

The phones went crazy. *Sports Illustrated* called. The Associated Press wanted confirmation of the story. It spread rapidly.

Although the news anchor and BBJ corrected the blunder after the commercial break, the "breaking story" had a life of its own. BBJ had to tape an apology that ran that night during the later newscasts because he had a few unscheduled days off—compliments of his dad.

BBJ would later laugh that he was half-right. He just had the date wrong. Barry Switzer would go on to coach the Dallas Cowboys in 1994—12 years after BBJ's April Fool's Day announcement.

Robert "Bob" Barry was inducted into the Oklahoma Journalism Hall of Fame in 1998. He died when he was 80 on October 30, 2011. Bob Barry, Jr. was inducted in 2016, a year after he died in a motorcycle accident.

MEMBERS INDUCTED IN THE 1990s

— 1990

Cullen Johnson (1901-1988), worked with the *Cheyenne Star* and the power centers in Washington, D.C., writer and editor in Seminole, Tonkawa, Alva, Mangum, and Elk City, worked with *The Daily Oklahoman* when it opened its Washington, D.C. news bureau in 1946.

Louise Beard Moore (1905-1992), reporter for the *Oklahoma News*, teacher for Oklahoma City Public Schools and Oklahoma City University, writer and city editor of the *Brownsville Herald* (Texas), supervisor of the *Oklahoma Daily* and Sooner yearbook at the University of Oklahoma.

Ray Parr (1910-1992), worked with *The Daily Oklahoman* for more than 40 years, state auditor, aide to the state welfare director, member of the Oklahoma City Gridiron Club, the National Press Club in Washington, and the Society of Professional Journalists.

Ernest A. Shiner (1927-1988), associate editor and editor for *Farmer-Stockman* Magazine, head of U.S. delegations to the World Congress of Agricultural Journalists in France (1971), chairman of the Oklahoma Farm Show, worked for the *Ada Evening News* and the *Weleetka American*.

Malvina Stephenson (1911-1996), Washington, D.C. correspondent, worked with the *Tulsa World* and other newspapers, international beat reporter, worked on the staff of U.S. Senator Robert S. Kerr for 13 years.

May Vandament (1891-1983), editor and publisher of the *Yukon Sun* with her husband, Poe, typesetter and then publisher of the *Bluejacket Gazette*, trained scores of young people in the printing trade and in newspaper work.

Poe B. Vandament (1883-1956), pioneer newspaper publisher, Oklahoma Hall of Fame inductee, editor and publisher of the *Yukon Sun* with his wife, May, mayor of Yukon, president of the Oklahoma Municipal League, president of the Oklahoma Press Association (1936).

H. Merle Woods (1894-1988), University of Oklahoma School of Journalism graduate (1907), news editor, then publisher and owner of the *EI Reno American*, president (1938) and treasurer of the Oklahoma Press Association, Oklahoma Hall of Fame inductee.

— 1991

Alex K. Adwan (1929-), Washington correspondent and editorial writer for the *Tulsa World*, recipient of the Bronze Star for combat heroism in the Korean War, United Press International Tulsa bureau manager, head of UPI operations in Houston and Oklahoma City.

James R. Campbell (1932-2018), worked with the *Bartlesville Examiner-Enterprise*, served in many capacities for United Press International in Oklahoma, Kansas, Arkansas, and Michigan, president of the Gridiron Club, Gridiron Foundation, the Press Club, and the Oklahoma chapter of the Society of Professional Journalists.

R. Jack Christy, Sr. (1901-1961), editor of the *Waukomis Hornet*, worked for 14 newspapers, including in Hollis, Mangum, Sayre, Hobart, Gotebo, Foss, Elk City, Watonga, EI Reno, and Enid.

Ivy M. Coffey (1917-2009), book page editor, food editor, women's editor, Sunday magazine writer, state staff reporter, and Washington, D.C. correspondent for *The Oklahoman* and *Oklahoma City Times*, worked as city editor for *Ponca City News*, covered Canadian County news for the *EI Reno Daily Tribune*.

William T. "Bill" Dixon (1921-2005), newspaper photography expert in Oklahoma for 40 years, chief photographer for *The Lawton Constitution* and *Morning Press*, freelance and commercial photographer.

Ken Neal (1935-), oil writer, church editor, state editor, copy editor, business editor, political reporter, and associate editor for the *Tulsa World*, recipient of a Phi Delta Kappa award, recognizing his "outstanding news media contribution to education."

Guy R. Old (1893-1986), linotype operator, then publisher for the *McCurtain Gazette* in Idabel, editor and publisher of the *Broken Bow News*, worked with the Oklahoma Corporation Commission.

Wava L. Denson Poindexter (1920-2006), publisher and co-owner of the *Gage Record* and *Ellis County Capital*, listed in *Who's Who of American Women*, member of the Oklahoma Press Association's Half Century Club, recipient of a citation from the Oklahoma State Senate in recognition of her contribution to journalism.

— **1992**

Warren F. Bickford III (1918-1980), reporter and eventually general manager of the *Blackwell Journal-Tribune*, president of the UPI Editors of Oklahoma, member of many committees for the Oklahoma Press Association.

Joseph H. Carter, Sr. (1932-), reporter for United Press International and the *Oklahoma Journal*, aide to congressmen and to Presidents Lyndon B. Johnson and Jimmy Carter, director of communications for the Democratic party, press secretary to Governor David Hall, vice president for public affairs at Cameron University, director of the Will Rogers Memorial, author of *Never Met a Man I Didn't Like: The Life and Writings of Will Rogers*.

Kay Dyer (1928-), first woman named city editor by the Oklahoma Publishing Company at *The Oklahoman* and the *Oklahoma City Times*, news editor, publisher, and editor for the *El Reno Daily Tribune*, recipient of a Ford Foundation Urban Journalism Fellowship.

M.C. Garber (1867-1948), lawyer, judge, mayor, congressman, and journalist, editor, and co-publisher of the consolidated *Enid Morning News* and *Enid Eagle* newspapers.

Mary Goddard (1924-1991), worked with *The Lawton Constitution*, Oklahoma State University's publications office, and *The Oklahoman* and *Oklahoma City Times*, teacher and writing coach for young journalists.

Donald J. Morrison (1913-1988), editor and publisher of his family's newspaper, the *Waurika News-Democrat*, from 1951 to 1981, using the paper's influence to lead the construction of Waurika Lake.

Mary Jo Nelson (1927-2007), editor and writer on such diverse beats as courthouse, city hall, state capitol, education, religion, business, and architecture for *The Oklahoman* and *Oklahoma City Times*.

 **Deacon New** (1925-1998), editor of the *Madill Record*, reporter and editor for the *Oklahoma City Times*, worked with the *Oil and Gas Journal* in Tulsa, oil editor, business editor, city editor, assistant managing editor and chief editorial writer for *The Daily Oklahoman*.

 **Joe W. Taylor** (1923-1978), worked with the *Haskell News* and daily newspapers in Corpus Christi, Texas and Alva, Oklahoma; published the *Hinton Record*, owner and co-publisher of *Davis News*, served in several positions for the Oklahoma Press Association.

— 1993

 **R. Marsden Bellatti** (1911-1981), worked with the *Blackwell Morning News*, held management positions at the *Stillwater News Press* and the *Nowata Daily Star*, served on the board of the Oklahoma Educational Television Authority, honored by the Oklahoma Press Association for 50 years in newspaper work.

 **John C. Casady** (1884-1965), editor and publisher of the *Cheyenne Star*, worked in print shops in Oklahoma, South Dakota, and Montana, grand master of the Odd Fellows Grand Lodge of Oklahoma, delegate to the Democratic National Convention.

 **Ruth Ferris** (1909-1998), worked with the *Altus Times Democrat, The Daily Oklahoman*, KOMA Radio in Oklahoma City, and KWHW in Altus, spent 20 years as public relations director for Altus Public Schools, established journalism certification for Oklahoma high schools.

 **John T. Greiner** (1942-), police, country, city hall, federal, and State Capitol beat reporter for *The Daily Oklahoman*, colonel in the U.S. Army Reserve, past president of the Oklahoma City Gridiron Club and the Gridiron Foundation.

 **Tony Hillerman** (1925-2008), worked for *The Lawton Constitution* and United Press in Oklahoma City, UP bureau manager and managing editor of the *Santa Fe New Mexican*, journalism professor and department head at The University of New Mexico, award-winning and best-selling author, president of Mystery Writers of America.

 **James J. Lange** (1926-2009), editorial cartoonist for *The Daily Oklahoman* for 58 years and artist of about 20,000 cartoons, founding member and president of American Editorial Cartoonists, president of the Oklahoma City Gridiron Club.

 **Jim Mayo** (1942-2019), publisher of the *Sallisaw Sequoyah County Times*, served in the U.S. Navy, president of the Oklahoma Press Association (1986), member of the National Newspaper Association and the International Society of Newspaper Editors.

 **Ted Ralston** (1918-1993), began his newspaper career as a high school student, worked as a newsman and editor his whole life except for military service time, trained many talented journalists who have worked at *The Lawton Constitution* and *Morning Press*.

Homer W. Ray (1929-2000), self-taught writer and editor, local editor and printer in his Texas hometown, recipient of many awards in journalism, co-owner of *Yale News* for 28 years with his wife, Beth.

— 1994

Eric Allen (1916-1986), president of Western Writers of America, author of 30 books, feature writer for many newspapers and magazines in Sallisaw, Muldrow, Alva, Enid, and Lawton as well as Fort Smith, Arkansas.

Jane Bryant (1933-2019), worked with the *Cushing Daily Citizen*, managing editor for the *Norman Transcript*, two-time head of the Oklahoma Associated Press Editors Association.

Ferdie J. Deering (1910-1993), worked at the *Ada Evening News* and the *Denison Herald*, worked with the Oklahoma Publishing Company for 48 years, editor of the *Farmer-Stockman*, president and trustee of the Southwest Livestock Association.

Edward L. Gaylord (1919-2003), editor and publisher of *The Daily Oklahoman*, which he considered to be his lifetime work and most important business enterprise, and leading supporter for a vast number of charitable and civic activities.

Joan E. Gilmore (1927-), news reporter, women's editor, and metropolitan editor for *The Daily Oklahoman*, public relations practitioner, weekly column writer for *The Journal Record*.

Stan Hoig (1924-2009), award-winning author, recipient of the Western Writers of America Golden Spur Award for Best Non-Fiction Book, journalism professor at the University of Central Oklahoma, Edmond Hall of Fame inductee.

Omer N. Schnoebelen (1912-2005), publisher, reporter, second-generation owner of the *Mooreland Leader*, Oklahoma Press Association Half Century Club member.

Margaret Taylor (1926-2005), co-owner and publisher of the *Davis News*, first female president of the Oklahoma Press Association (1990), leased the *Hinton Record* with her husband, Joe Taylor.

F.E. "Wally" Wallis (1907-1981), *The Oklahoman* and *Oklahoma City Times* sportswriter for 27 years, known as the state's foremost golf authority, president of the Golf Writers Association of America and the Oklahoma City Press Club.

W.P. "Bill" Atkinson (1906-1999), journalist, builder, educator, and politician, founder of the *Oklahoma Journal*, head of the Oklahoma City University Journalism Department, president of the National Association of Home Builders, often regarded as the founder of Midwest City.

Donovan Banzett (1903-1983), owner and publisher of several newspapers, active member in church and civic affairs, founder of the *Edmond Booster*, which he printed for 20 years, at first in his mother's kitchen.

James W. Bradshaw (1923-2006), Oklahoma newspaper writer and editor for 43 years, 39 of them at the *Shawnee News-Star*, covering courtroom dramas, fires, floods, elections, labor disputes, and industrial plants.

Klina E. Casady (1891-1981), co-publisher with her husband, John Casady, of the *Cheyenne Star*, founder of the first 4-H Club in her county, member of the Oklahoma Press Association's Half Century Club.

Paul English (1937-2016), worked with the *Duncan Banner*, the United Press International, and *The Oklahoman*, reporter at the State Capitol, covering the terms of seven governors, president of the Oklahoma Chapter of the Society of Professional Journalists.

Marlan Dee Nelson (1934-), writer, managing editor, and editor for the *Haskell News*, director of the Oklahoma State University School of Journalism and Broadcasting, administrator and professor at Southern Illinois University and Utah State.

Max J. Nichols (1934-), sportswriter for *The Oklahoman*, award-winning writer, editor, and columnist for the *Minneapolis Star*, national president of the Baseball Writers Association of America, editor and columnist for *The Journal Record*, journalism professor at Oklahoma City University, author of a double biography on John and Eleanor Kirkpatrick.

Omer F. Schnoebelen (1884-1972), printer and editor for 69 years, founder of the *Mooreland Leader* at age 19, member of the Oklahoma Press Association's Half Century Club.

Milo W. Watson (1917-1998), newspaperman in Oklahoma for more than a half century, publisher of the *Perry Daily Journal*, president of the Oklahoma Press Association (1967), named Perry's Outstanding Citizen (1982), mentor for young writers and editors.

Charles Robert Bellatti (1886-1953), publisher in Blackwell, consolidated two Stillwater papers in 1941 to form the *Stillwater News Press*, founder of Stillwater's first radio station, KSPI-AM, later bringing KSPI-FM on the air in 1951 as one of the first FM stations west of the Mississippi.

John Clabes (1929-), worked for papers in Hobart and Lawton, managing editor and editor of the *Oklahoma Journal*, public affairs officer of the Southwest Region of the Federal Aviation Administration in Fort Worth, Texas and of the Mike Monroney Aeronautical Center in Oklahoma City.

Gene Curtis (1929-), joined the *Tulsa World* in 1948 while a student at The University of Tulsa, worked with the paper for the next 46 years, with the exception of two years during the Korean War.

Robert E. Lee (1931-2014), worked for the *Harper County Journal*, held managerial positions in Woodward and Enid as well as at *The Oklahoman*, wrote columns three days a week for *The Oklahoman*, volunteered with Lions Club International.

Robert E. Lorton (1937-), publisher of the *Tulsa World*, chairman and chief executive officer of World Publishing Company, working in every major department of the paper, active community leader, and philanthropist.

Paul S. McClung (1924-2007), executive editor of *The Lawton Constitution* and *Morning Press*, director of information at Cameron University, writer for national magazines, Southwest Bureau Chief for Dell Publishing Company, Army veteran of World War II.

Jim Monroe (1925-2015), worked on several Oklahoma dailies, worked with the New York City AP Bureau, executive director of the Oklahoma Democratic Party, worked on the staff of Senator Fred Harris in Washington, D.C., published the *McCurtain Gazette* in Idabel.

Ted M. Phillips (1932-2004), second-generation editor of the *Seminole Producer*, Army veteran, 38-year member of Kiwanis, elder in the Presbyterian Church, chairman of the Seminole Junior College Board of Regents, president (1989) and treasurer of the Oklahoma Press Association.

Albert Riesen, Jr. (1932-2012), co-publisher and publisher of the *Daily Ardmoreite* in Ardmore, served in the Air Force, involved with management of KVSO Radio and KVSO-TV, board member of the Southern Newspaper Publishers Association.

James C. Argo (1938-2017), international, national, regional, and state award-winning photojournalist, capturing by word and film the images of joy and despair that comprise life in Oklahoma.

Frank Boggs (1928-2017), sports editor and columnist, named six times as outstanding sportswriter in Oklahoma, worked for the *Topeka Daily Capital, San Diego Evening Tribune* and *Oklahoma City Times*, managing editor of *The Oklahoman*.

Jack Bowen (1947-), news anchor for KOCO-TV, KWTV, and KOKH Channel 25, active in community activities, sought to provide impact in Oklahoma in a positive way.

William Bryan Connors, Jr. (1931-2000), sports editor of the *Tulsa World* for nearly three decades, honored many times as Oklahoma's outstanding sportswriter, sports editor of the *Stillwater News Press*, sports staffer on *The Oklahoman*.

Ronald L. Jenkins (1944-), sports editor for his hometown daily in Fort Smith, Arkansas, worked with the *Oklahoma Journal*, capitol correspondent for The Associated Press in Oklahoma City, familiar face on OETA's weekly legislative review show.

Edith Cherry Johnson (1879-1961), reporter and columnist for *The Daily Oklahoman* for more than a half century, winning considerable acclaim for a column that ran on the editorial page for 44 years, author, active member in her community.

James Stewart, Sr. (1912-1997), columnist and editorial writer for *The Black Dispatch* in Oklahoma City, active in the civil rights movement, president of the Oklahoma Natural Gas Company, Oklahoma Hall of Fame inductee.

William Stanley "Bill" Tharp, Sr. (1914-1996), respected journalist in Oklahoma for more than 40 years, teacher and coach, worked with the *Henryetta Daily Free-Lance*, associate editor of *The Oklahoma Journal*, weekly columnist for the *Midwest City Sun*.

John R. Whitaker (1906-1978), professor at the University of Oklahoma School of Journalism, University of Missouri, and University of Houston and Syracuse, Fulbright lecturer in Peru and Bolivia, worked with Denver, Colorado, St. Louis, Missouri, and EI Paso, Texas newspapers and for the United Press.

Robert "Bob" Barry (1931-2011), sports director and sportscaster for KFOR-TV, worked at KNOR in Norman, served on the National Sportscasters Association Board of Directors, elected Oklahoma Sportscaster of the Year 15 times.

Linda Cavanaugh (1950-), worked at KFOR-TV Channel 4 in Oklahoma City for more than 20 years, became the state's first female co-anchor in 1979, recipient of more than 30 national awards, 40 regional and state awards, and 11 Emmys.

Reba N. Collins (1925-2005), national speaker and author, recognized as the foremost Will Rogers scholar, professor and public relations professional at Central State University, director of the Will Rogers Memorial.

D. Jo Ferguson (1922-2010), publisher of the *Pawnee Chief*, president of the Oklahoma Press Association (1972), recipient of the Milt Phillips Award (1993), correspondent in the Navy, sending nearly 1,000 stories back to hometown newspapers during World War II.

Fred H. Grove (1913-2008), editor, University of Oklahoma press relations writer, journalism teacher, OETA staff writer, western fiction and historical author, worked with the *Cushing Daily Citizen*, the *Shawnee Evening Star*, *Oklahoma City Times* and *The Daily Oklahoman*, recipient of a National Cowboy & Western Heritage Museum award for his novel, *The Buffalo Runners*.

Marie Price (1947-), managing editor of Oklahoma City University's student newspaper, *The Campus*; covered state politics for 30 years, Capitol Bureau Chief of the *Oklahoma Legislative Reporter*, writer for *The Journal Record*.

Walter N. Radmilovich, Jr. (1930-2008), public relations practitioner and vice president of corporate communications for the Oklahoma Natural Gas Company, worked with the *EI Reno American*, reporter-photographer for the *EI Reno Tribune*, assistant oil editor of *The Daily Oklahoman*, business editor of the *Tulsa World*, named Tulsa Public Relations Professional of the Year in 1981.

Arthur B. Ramsey (1914-2000), pioneer Oklahoma newsreel cameraman, filmed the news events of The Depression for Pathe, Paramount, and Fox Movietone, including interviews with Will Rogers and Governor William H. "Alfalfa Bill" Murray, served in the Army as head of all combat camera units (1943).

William P. Ross (1820-1891), chief of the Cherokee Nation, founder and editor of the *Cherokee Advocate*, edited the *Indian Journal* at Eufaula, the *Indian Chieftain*, and the *Indian Arrow*, lieutenant colonel in the Army of the Confederacy.

— 1999

Claude V. Barrow (1896-1978), considered a pioneer in the field of petroleum press, oil editor for *The Daily Oklahoman* for 35 years, worked with newspapers in Hugo, Ardmore, Tulsa, and Texas, community leader.

Jack Brannan (1936-2014), journalist and public relations specialist, worked with United Press International, *Joplin Globe, Tulsa World*, New York Stock Exchange, *Los Angeles Times,* and as a foreign correspondent overseas.

M.J. Van Deventer (1940-), freelance writer, director of publications for the National Cowboy Hall of Fame, editor of *Persimmon Hill* Magazine, lifestyle and entertainment editor for the *Stillwater News Press*, worked with the *Tulsa World, Fort Worth Star Telegram,* and *The Daily Oklahoman*, editor of *Oklahoma Home & Lifestyle Magazine, Tulsa Magazine,* and *Tulsa Lifestyle*, director of publications for the Color Graphics Corporation in Tulsa.

Lucia Loomis Ferguson (1887-1962), assistant editor of the *Cherokee Republican*, columnist for Scripps-Howard newspapers, wrote for the *Tulsa Tribune*, the *Times-Press* in Akron, Ohio, the *Rocky Mountain News* and *Fort Worth Press*, vice president of the Oklahoma Press Association and the League of American Pen Women.

Dennie Hall (1934-), teacher, reporter, editor, and public relations practitioner, co-founder of the Oklahoma Journalism Hall of Fame, general assignments reporter at *EI Dorado News-Times* (Arkansas), editor for the *Plaines Daily Quill* (Missouri) and the *Nashville Banner*, professor at the University of Central Oklahoma, faculty adviser of *The Vista*.

Philip Morris (1940-2017), building editor and editor-at-large for the *Southern Living* Magazine group, Oklahoma reporter, national honorary member of the American Institute of Architects and the American Society of Landscape Architects.

Gaylord Shaw (1942-2015), Pulitzer Prize winner, senior correspondent in *Newsday's* Washington Bureau, reporter and editor for the *Los Angeles Times* and *Dallas Times Herald*, correspondent for The Associated Press.

George F. Tapscott (1914-2002), assistant chief photographer for *The Daily Oklahoman*, combat photographer for the *45th Division News* during World War II, member of the National Guard.

Riley Ward Wilson (1929-2007), reporter for the *Shawnee News-Star*, editor, business-oil editor, and general editor at the *Tulsa World*.

2000 - 2009
the decade for community and more women journalists

The new millennium featured a Hall of Fame journalist with a story about how she overcame discrimination against women in the 1950s. She walked away from a job to do it.

Katherine Hatch, reporter, foreign correspondent, and author, worked at *TIME* Magazine in New York but left in 1959 "because women weren't offered writing jobs." She was the only woman inducted in the 2000 Millennium Class of the Oklahoma Journalism Hall of Fame, but 27 others would join her during the decade.

As fellow 2000 inductee Terry Clark would write later, "The members of the Oklahoma Journalism Hall of Fame's 'Millennial Generation' weren't young. Two of those inducted in 2000 as the hall approached its twentieth anniversary were posthumous, and the other seven had gray hair."

Clark is the only Oklahoma Journalism Hall of Fame Director inducted while holding the position. Besides being an educator, Clark was a community journalist, having owned the *Waurika News-Democrat* for 12 years.

Community journalists were a hallmark of the decade. They included Roy Angel, who spent his entire 35-year career as sports editor of the *Shawnee News-Star*. He worked with Hall of Famers Jim and Virginia Bradshaw, Mike McCormick, and Joe Hight. Of the 90 inducted that decade, many were like Angel in rural and small-city publications. Maebeth "Beth" Ray was one. By the time she was inducted in 2001, she had worked 68 years in community journalism since the age of six. Her father, Ralph E. Cain, and husband Homer Ray also were Hall of Famers.

Others inducted during the decade include *Today Show* co-anchor Jim Hartz; Bob Burke, who may be the most prolific nonfiction writer in history; broadcast pioneers Pam Henry and Billie Rodely; Freedom of Information Oklahoma founder and online innovator Sue Hale; famed photographer David Fitzgerald; investigative journalist Terri Watkins, the first woman in Oklahoma City Gridiron; Oklahoma Press Association head Mark Thomas, longtime emcee of the Hall of Fame ceremonies; Oklahoma AP Bureau Chief and Freedom of Information Oklahoma founder Lindel Hutson; *The Black Chronicle* founder Russell Perry; and the husband-wife super-journalist team of Gloria and Wayne Trotter.

The first Posthumous Award of Membership was awarded to eight journalists in 2005. They were Doris Hedges, Vera Holding, Ben Langdon, Eugene Lorton, Joseph W. Miller, Alexander L. Posey, Wayne Singleterry, and Tom Steed. Steed was a nationally recognized congressman who also had a long career in journalism.

Many of them also were community journalists.

Helen Ford Wallace interviews Vicki Gourley, Joan Gilmore, and Peggy Gandy on a Parties Extra web cast.

Debbie Jackson with former Oklahoma Governor George Nigh. Courtesy of the *Tulsa World*.

Patrick O'Dell covered national stories about Oklahoma for more than three decades as a CBS Southwest Bureau cameraman. In 1961 he graduated from The University of Tulsa, beginning his career at KOTV.

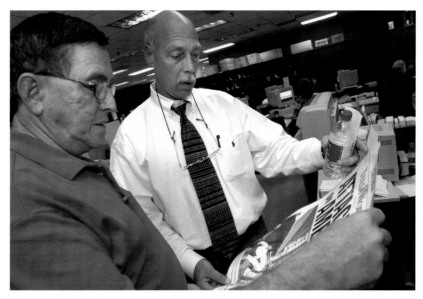

Joe Worley and Bill Harper look over the special section published by the *Tulsa World* following the terrorist attacks on the United States on September 11, 2001. Photo by John Clanton. Courtesy of the *Tulsa World*.

Over 29 years, AP's Lewis Ferguson covered six Kansas governors, 29 legislative sessions, and nine national political conventions. Here he is pictured inside the Kansas State Capitol. Date unknown.

Bill Harper and prepress staff members work on the *Tulsa World's* special edition on the terrorist attacks on New York and Washington, D.C. on Tuesday, September 11, 2001. Photo by David Crenshaw. Courtesy of the *Tulsa World*.

Tulsa resident Bob Haring surveys the damage to his backyard and his neighbor's (background) as he stands in Maple Park. At least two cottonwoods came down and took out fence and backyard structures such as a doghouse and the brown structure in the rear. Photo by Robert S. Cross. June 2, 2004. Courtesy of the *Tulsa World*.

Bill Harper yells to fellow officials during the 2007 OCA All-State football game at Moore High School on July 27, 2007. Photo by Joey Johnson. Courtesy of the *Tulsa World*.

The *Tulsa World's* Bob Haring (left), Sid Steen (center), and Bob Lorton. 1975. Courtesy of the *Tulsa World*.

Sunday Editor Debbie Jackson during a daily budget meeting at the *Tulsa World* on Thursday, December 28, 2017. Photo by Jessie Wardarski. Courtesy of the *Tulsa World*.

Joe Worley reads pages from the *Tulsa World's* special edition on terrorist attacks on New York and Washington, D.C. on September 11, 2001. Photo by David Crenshaw. Courtesy of the *Tulsa World*.

Joe Worley addresses the staff following the *Tulsa World's* publication of a special section on September 11, 2001, the day that terrorists struck the United States. Photo by Tom Gilbert. Courtesy of the *Tulsa World*.

Governor Frank Keating speaks with the *Tulsa World's* Joe Worley after the Oklahoma City bombing in April 1995. Photo by Tom Gilbert. Courtesy of the *Tulsa World*.

Jeff Dixon began his photography career at *The Lawton Constitution/Morning Press* in high school in 1965. He has won numerous awards from the Oklahoma Press Association and the Associated Press; in 2006, the Lawton Arts and Humanities Council named him Artist of the Year.

After almost a three-month delay because of the General Motors auto workers' strike, all five new Moore garbage trucks have arrived. Inspecting are, from left, Harold Crow, sanitation superintendent; Jim Grider, foreman; and Early English, city manager. December 9, 1970, *Oklahoman Times*. Joe Miller photo. Courtesy of the Oklahoma Historical Society.

Fred Marvel, Oklahoma Department of Tourism and Recreation photographer, covers the state of Oklahoma. Photo by Jim Argo. March 6, 2000.

Oklahoma Sooners are on the move in this George R. Wilson photo dated September 8, 1984. Oklahoma Publishing Co. Courtesy of the Oklahoma Historical Society.

A runaway wheel struck this window at the Circle Furniture Co., 5101 Classen Blvd. Wednesday afternoon and store manager Royce Ewing surveys the damage. November 18, 1964. *The Daily Oklahoman*. Joe Miller photo. Courtesy of the Oklahoma Historical Society.

Berry Tramel (right) interviews Blake Griffin at *The Oklahoman's* 2019 Prep Sports Awards banquet. Courtesy of *The Oklahoman*.

SPORTSWRITERS
speaking the state's language
By Berry Tramel, 2018 Inductee

I walked into the Shawnee High School football press box in 1980 as a 19-year-old reporter who didn't know a deadline from a dateline. I met the old guy covering the Shawnee Wolves.

Roy Angel. I didn't know I was in the presence of a legend. I know it now.

Angel, the 35-year sports editor (1949-84) of the *Shawnee News-Star*, was inducted into the Oklahoma Journalism Hall of Fame in 2000.

Over the next four decades, I would count Ray Soldan and Dave Sittler as staff colleagues, and Bill Connors and John Klein as press box contemporaries. In fact, among the sportswriters in the Hall of Fame, only one, John Cronley, did I never get to know. And in April 2018, I joined their ranks in the Hall of Fame, an incredible honor, considering what sportswriters have meant to Oklahomans.

My dad, a sharecropper's son during the Depression, would wait by the train tracks in the Ozark foothills of Mayes County, waiting for the eastbound train to drop off a bundle of the *Tulsa World*. Dad would unwrap the bundle, pull out a newspaper, and read the likes of B.A. Bridgewater, before tucking the paper back into the bundle to be spread to paying customers. Eventually, my dad became a subscriber to four newspapers a day that I grew up reading.

Sports, then and now, is a state language. Be it the St. Louis Cardinals and the baseball town teams of the state's early days, or Bud Wilkinson's Sooners and Henry Iba's Aggies from the post-war era, or the modern-day exploits of the Thunder, University of Oklahoma, and Oklahoma State University, sports bring Oklahomans together. And the honored scribes and many more have been instrumental in fostering celebrations and debates and memories of Oklahoma sports over the last century-plus.

It's like the famed Red Smith once said. "People go to the ballpark to have fun, then pick up the paper the next morning to have fun all over again."

That's what people like Hall of Famers Frank Boggs, Ray Soldan, Dave Sittler, John Cronley, William Bryan Connors, Jr., John Klein, and B.A. Bridgewater have done in the major metros. Likewise, Angel is the patron saint of the community newspaper sports editors in Oklahoma, but Jim Weeks at the *Norman Transcript*, Joey Goodman and Herb Jacobs at *The Lawton Constitution*, Jim Ellis at the *Miami News-Record*, Jeff Cali at the *Ada Evening News*, Bruce Campbell at the *Enid News & Eagle*, Ron Holt at the *Stillwater News Press,* and Fred Fehr at the *Shawnee News-Star* all have done the invaluable work of feeding Oklahomans' insatiable desire to read about their sporting heroes.

As a kid, I read those kinds of journalists. As a young professional, I followed those kinds of journalists. At age 58, entering my 42nd football season in the business, I stand proudly beside those kinds of journalists.

And I cherish the memories of the Hall of Famers.

Soldan, with his uncommon devotion to history. Connors, with his unmatched record of trust with our state's most prominent coaches. Cronley, with his turning of the phrase. Sittler, with his dogged reporting.

And man, the stories. Back in 1984, I was sick as a dog, but we were short-handed at the *Transcript*. I covered Wayman Tisdale's announcement that he would return for a third season at OU, then went across the street to cover a Sooner baseball doubleheader. In the Mitchell Park press box, I lost my lunch and sprinted to a trash can in the back of the room to throw up. Just then, John Klein arrived. He walked through the door and without breaking stride looked at me and said, "My sentiments exactly."

I remember calling Ray Soldan in 2000 for an *Oklahoman* project, asking who was the greatest high school player he had ever seen. By then, Soldan had covered a half-century of Oklahoma high school football.

Soldan selected Wes Welker, a contemporary pick from Oklahoma City's Heritage Hall. I was skeptical, because our panel had selected all kinds of historical players. But Soldan was adamant that Welker was the best. And a few years later, when Welker was Tom Brady's favorite target with the New England Patriots, Soldan stood on the solid rock of truth.

I remember a drive to Springfield, Missouri, with Bill Connors for an OSU game, a quick trip to the Ozarks that was filled with stories of our state's most legendary sportsmen, from Bud Wilkinson to Eddie Sutton.

And I remember a television feature on Frank Boggs, when he was retired, in which he mentioned that I was one of the writers he liked to read. I felt stunned that a writer of Boggs' skill would say such a thing. To be included with such Hall of Fame company is something I never dreamed.

We all got into the business because it was fun. Even when it turned serious, it remained fun. Still is fun. But it's also important, because such sportswriters have brought Oklahomans together daily, in the marketplace of shared memories.

John Cronley was inducted into the Oklahoma Journalism Hall of Fame in 1974, Frank Boggs in 1997, Ray Soldan in 2009, Dave Sittler in 2005, William Bryan Connors, Jr. in 1997, John Klein in 2013, and B.A. Bridgewater in 2020. Berry Tramel nominated Bridgewater after realizing that he wasn't in the Hall of Fame while writing this story.

Hall of Famer Jim Hartz served as a longtime chairman of the Will Rogers Memorial Commission. Photo courtesy of Joseph H. Carter, Sr. collection.

"Ray Soldan has covered nearly 1,000 high school football games for *The Oklahoman*." Creator unknown. 1991. Courtesy of the Oklahoma Historical Society.

JIM HARTZ
from an Oklahoma twang to Today Show host
By Joseph H. Carter, Sr., 1992 Inductee

Tulsa Drillers Director of Public/Media Relations Brian Carroll (left) and *Tulsa World* reporter John Klein (right) help longtime head usher for the Drillers Harry Brook out of a car at ONEOK Field in Tulsa, Oklahoma. March 28, 2017. Photo by James Gibbard. Courtesy of the *Tulsa World*.

Born in 1940, Jim Hartz was the son of an Assembly of God pastor. He and I were young newsmen when I first met him in Tulsa. Later, we co-owned a public affairs consultancy in Washington, D.C.

To pay tuition as a pre-medicine major at The University of Tulsa, Hartz found part-time work as a radio announcer at KOME Radio. There, a talented producer transformed his Oklahoma twang into a broadcast-quality voice that would soon echo around the world. To the chagrin of his assistant police chief brother, Hartz never became a doctor.

From KOME Hartz moved to KRMG Radio news and finally to KOTV, Tulsa's new CBS-TV affiliate. Hartz rose from a TV street reporter to news director in just two years.

In 1962 a roving talent scout for NBC-TV stopped by Tulsa, watched the local news, and suggested that the nation's top network audition Hartz, who was anchoring two newscasts.

He was hired at 24 as NBC-TV's youngest news correspondent ever. For more than a decade, Hartz was news anchor at 6:00 p.m. and 11:00 p.m. at the network's local affiliate in New York City. He captured a top Q rating in America's largest city, reflecting popularity greater than the fame of Mayor John Lindsay.

Hartz was often dispatched on assignments, including many space shots, wars, and celebrity interviews. While covering a war in Israel, his unit was targeted by artillery fire but was saved by ducking into a bunker.

During a perilous space flight that Hartz anchored for NBC-TV, the producer walked onto the set during a station break and whispered: "Our survey shows 250 million people are watching you, Jim." Stage lights went up and the boy from north Tulsa swallowed surprise and resumed reporting professionally.

Upon joining NBC, Shawnee, Oklahoma-born, and equally famous Hall of Fame newsman Frank McGee became Hartz's "guru," giving sage advice about network politics, agents, and performance.

Hartz once said McGee advised him that anchoring space shots required three things: the anchor must be able to ad-lib endlessly. Have a tough butt. And own a huge bladder.

For two years, Hartz served as co-host of the *Today Show*. When fellow *Today Show* star Barbara Walters left NBC for ABC, Hartz requested a return to pure journalism and was assigned as the main news anchor at WRC-TV, NBC's station in Washington, D.C.

Hartz interviewed multiple presidents, politicos, heads of states, and corporate chiefs in addition to anchoring hundreds of newscasts with top ratings.

Among other honors, Hartz won five Emmy Awards and two Ace Awards.

For decades public television enlisted Hartz, including as *Over Easy* co-host with actress Mary Martin, host of Tokyo-produced *Asia Now,* and of *Innovation*, a series devoted to scientific research.

Hartz delved deeply into space science, being the first reporter to fly in the supersonic spy plane, the SR-71, and other high-performance planes. His scientific knowledge led to authoring the alarming and instructive book *Worlds Apart* with Astronaut Rich Chapel. The book explored the tragic lack of clear communications between scientists and journalists. Hartz also wrote freelance articles for *Reader's Digest* and *National Geographic.*

Governor Henry Bellmon appointed Hartz to Oklahoma's Will Rogers Memorial Commission and Senator Stratton Taylor led the confirmation. With later reappointments, Hartz served for decades as the active chairman.

Hartz retired at his Alexandria, Virginia home that was built in the seventeenth century.

Married to Alexandra Hartz, Hartz fathered a son and two daughters.

Frank McGee was inducted into the Oklahoma Journalism Hall of Fame in 1974. He was followed in 2003 by Jim Hartz. Joseph H. Carter, Sr. and Jim Hartz have remained friends through the years.

IDA B BLACKBURN
my mom: a pioneer in television
By Bob Blackburn, 2020 Lifetime Achievement Recipient

There will never be another Ida B.

From 1958 to 1975, Ida B. Blackburn hosted more than 3,000 shows on live television at KOCO-TV in Oklahoma City.

Following that remarkable run on the air, Ida B became the first female sales executive at a television station in the state, opened the first advertising agency in the state owned by a woman, and earned a reputation as a concert promoter with clients from Eddie Arnold and Liza Minnelli to Sonny and Cher.

It all began in Ninnekah, Oklahoma, a small rural community in Grady County where she was born in 1929. With a father in the oil patch, the family moved to Cement, Chickasha, and Chandler, where Ida B graduated from high school.

Her college training as a music teacher started at the Oklahoma College for Women, known today as the University of Science and Arts of Oklahoma, and concluded at Central State College, how the University of Central Oklahoma. Then came marriage, a short teaching career, and two children, Bobby (me) and Betty.

Ida B started her television career in 1958 when she auditioned for the role as host of a pre-school children's show called *Romper Room*. Later shows, usually 30-minute live broadcasts in the morning, were called *At Home with Ida B, Dateline Hollywood,* and *The Ida B Show.* Typically, her shows featured community events, entertainment, and organizations that had a message to share with the general public.

Her lively personality, paired with a quick wit and a gift at drawing information from guests who usually were nervous about appearing on television, kept her on the air until 1975 when *Good Morning America* took the morning time slot.

Ida B used the medium of television to make a difference in the community. She hosted minority guests when Oklahoma City was still segregated by race.

She gave many artists such as Anthony Armstrong Jones and Jody Miller a chance to appear on television for the first time. And along with Rex Reed, she was one of the first local market television personalities in the country to regularly attend movie premieres and promotional events that had long been the domain of print journalists.

For many people who grew up in central Oklahoma in the 1960s

and 1970s, Ida B was a daily guest in their homes and a source for what was going on in their community. For my sister, Betty, and me, Ida B was also a mother, a mentor, and a daily reminder that talent might be important, but the real test of a person's ability comes down to hard work, creativity, and overcoming the obstacles that come our way.

For us, she was Mom and a source of constant love. For everyone else, she was Ida B.

Ida B. was inducted into the Oklahoma Journalism Hall of Fame in 2001. She died in 2016 at 87. Bob Blackburn, Executive Director of the Oklahoma Historical Society, was recognized with the Lifetime Achievement Award for his contributions to journalism in 2020.

As the host for more than 3,000 live television shows, Ida B created another outlet for news about events, organizations, and businesses. Here, she is a good sport demonstrating a new Daisy BB gun. Photo courtesy of the Oklahoma Historical Society.

Ida Blackburn, better known as Ida B, hosted a daily television show at KOCO-TV in Oklahoma City from 1958 to 1975. Here, she sits at the control booth where her director sat during the shows. Photo courtesy of the Oklahoma Historical Society.

HEDGES, HOLDING, LANGDON, LORTON, MILLER, POSEY, SINGLETERRY, STEED
honoring the first posthumous award of membership class

The first Posthumous Award of Membership was bestowed in 2005 to six men and two women who had distinguished careers in Oklahoma journalism history.

They included a longtime reporter, photographer, newspaper owners, and publishers, two journalists who became poets, and a journalist who became a United States congressman and now has a highway and lake in Oklahoma named after him.

It wouldn't be until 2020 when the second Posthumous Award of Membership would be awarded to 10 journalists.

Even though only two posthumous classes have been selected, the Hall of Fame has inducted deceased journalists among its regular classes in its 50-year history. Only two, Edward King Gaylord and H.H. Herbert, were living when the first induction was announced in 1971. By the induction announcement a year later, seven of the nine honorees were living. Since then, most journalists selected for induction were living at the time of the announcement.

One, publisher Ray Lokey, was told that he would be inducted in 2018 just days before his death on November 11, 2017.

In 2005, it was decided that on special occasions a posthumous class would be named with the yearly class.

These are the distinguished journalists in the first class:

Doris Hedges (1910-1999), co-publisher of the *Lawton Morning Press* and co-owner of the *Eufaula Indian Journal* with her husband, Homer, managing editor of the *Tahlequah Star Citizen*, an active member of the Oklahoma Press Association, award-winning columnist.

Vera Holding (1894-1984), published four poetry books, editor of the *Tipton Tribune*, *Waurika News-Democrat*, and *Comanche Reflex*, worked with the *Duncan Banner*, correspondent for *The Daily Oklahoman*, *Lawton Press*, and the *Wichita Falls Record News and Times*, co-owner of the *Potter County News* (Texas).

Ben Langdon (1913-1999), published *The Magnum Star* for 33 years with his wife, Betty, served in the U.S. Army in World War II, president of the Oklahoma Press Association (1970), director of the Oklahoma Industrial Development board, senior staff member for Governor George Nigh.

Eugene Lorton (1869-1949), worked with the *Medicine Lodge Cressett*, *Salubria Citizen*, and *Boise City Sentinel*, established the *Emmet Index*, owner of the *Mound City Republic*, managing editor of the *Walla Walla Union*, established the *Washtucna Enterprise*, owner of the *Tulsa World*.

Joseph W. Miller (1921-1992), worked with *The Daily Oklahoman* and *Oklahoma City Times*, covering the home front during World War II and photographing the rise of OU football, mentor to many young photographers.

Alexander L. Posey (1873-1908), Creek Nation Bard and poet laureate, helped publish *The Instructor* at Bacone College, superintendent of public instruction for the Creek Nation, editor of the *Eufaula Indian Journal* and the *Muskogee Times*, publisher of the *Indian Journal*.

Wayne Singleterry (1949-2001), worked 20 years for *The Daily Oklahoman* as reporter and assistant city editor, covering city hall; worked on the *Oklahoma Daily* and the *Norman Transcript*.

Tom Steed (1904-1983), U.S. Congressman, worked with the *Ada Evening News*, correspondent for *The Daily Oklahoman*, reporter for the *Bartlesville Examiner-Enterprise*, telegraph editor for the *McAlester News-Capital*, news editor and managing editor for the *Shawnee News-Star*.

THE POWER COUPLES OF OKLAHOMA JOURNALISM
most represent print, except for the "co-anchors for life"
By Billie Rodely, 2004 Inductee

The number of journalists joined in marriage is more common than you would think, especially if you look at the Oklahoma Journalism Hall of Fame. Twelve couples are now in the Hall of Fame. Most represent print media.

Except for Jim and me.

Jim Palmer and I were inducted one year apart and now are the only broadcast couple in the Hall of Fame. Jim is a native Oklahoman, but began his radio career in Wisconsin, before quickly returning home from the cold North to work in news at various Oklahoma radio stations. I began in Indianapolis. Kansas City was my next radio news stop before I moved to Oklahoma City and worked for KTOK-AM. We met when Jim was hired as news director at KTOK, and I was assistant news director. Both of us have decades of experience reporting, editing, and anchoring. And, most importantly, we married in 1995 and became "co-anchors for life."

Poe B. Vandament and May Vandament each spent more than five decades in publishing and newspaper work. Before publishing the *Yukon Sun* with her husband, May was with the *Bluejacket Gazette*. Poe came to Oklahoma before statehood and published many papers before the *Yukon Sun*. Although the *Sun* was sold in 1948, May remained on staff working and mentoring. Poe's service to journalism, as well as civic and community affairs, earned him induction into the Oklahoma Hall of Fame in 1949.

J. Leland Gourley was an award-winning editor and publisher long before he launched *FRIDAY*, an Oklahoma City suburban weekly newspaper, in 1974. He hired Vicki Clark that same year to cover The Village. Her father was mayor of The Village at the time. The couple married in 1976. J. Leland Gourley died in 2013 and Vicki Gourley continues as the owner and publisher of Nichols Hills Publishing and *FRIDAY*.

Alfred W. McLaughlin was a renowned photographer. He and Joan E. Gilmore met at *The Daily Oklahoman*, where collectively they worked for more than 65 years. Among McLaughlin's many awards was the National Women's Page Photographer of the Year. Gilmore served as women's editor of the newspaper. Together, they forged a video production and public relations business which included memorializing several Oklahoma Gridiron Shows. McLaughlin died in 2013. Gilmore continues to write and report and is an avid community volunteer.

John D. and Gracie Montgomery are co-publishers of the *Purcell Register*. John's work in the newspaper business began in his hometown at the *Hobart Daily Democrat-Chief* and the *Kiowa County Star-Review*. Gracie's journalism career started at the *Johnston County Capital-Democrat*. Both have served tirelessly on every committee of the Oklahoma Press Association and are the first husband-and-wife team to have served as OPA president. The Montgomery family is active in the civic and cultural life of Purcell and McClain County.

Michael R. "Mick" Hinton and Sue Brewster Hinton both became interested in journalism as students at the University of Oklahoma. They were married in 1968. Mick's work includes the *Oklahoma City Times, The Daily Oklahoman,* and the *Norman Transcript*. Sue has worked for the *Norman Transcript* and *The Oklahoman*. The Hintons share a devotion to education, as Mick covered education for *The Daily Oklahoman,* and Sue taught journalism at Oklahoma City Community College. She was the first to receive the College's President's Award for Excellence in Teaching.

Bill and Barbara Walter owned and operated the *Hennessey Clipper* and were inducted into the Hall of Fame in 2008. They were fixtures at nearly all Oklahoma Press Association functions. Bill was a third-generation publisher of the *Clipper*, which had been in his family since 1904. Bill died in 2017.

The co-publishers of *The Countywide News & Sun* are Gloria and Wayne Trotter. Gloria's professional experience isn't limited to print journalism, as she includes television and radio news in her resume. Wayne's history includes work for newspapers in Mississippi, Virginia, and North Carolina. In 1983, the pair took on the *Tecumseh Countywide News* then founded, and ultimately combined, *The Shawnee Sun* into *The Countywide & Sun* in 2008. Wayne has numerous awards for his editorials and columns. Both are past presidents of the Oklahoma Press Association.

John M. Wylie II and Faith L. Wylie might be considered a journalism "power couple." Like most of the Hall of Fame couples, the Wylies have garnered numerous awards and accolades during their careers. They purchased the *Oologah Lake Leader* in 1984 and moved from the Kansas City area, where John worked for the *Kansas City Star* and was part of a Pulitzer Prize-winning reporting team. Both are well-known for their passionate pursuit of investigative reporting and adherence to Freedom of Information and Open Meetings/Open Records laws.

Virginia Bradshaw and Jim Bradshaw met at the *Shawnee News-Star* when she asked him if he knew of any summer jobs. He didn't, but instead asked her on a date. They were married for 55 years. Jim spent 39 of his 43-year career working for the *News-Star*, 14 years as managing editor. The stories he covered included courtroom dramas, fires, floods, elections, and labor disputes. He crusaded for improvements through his column "From This Moment." Virginia's standout career included writing two books and 26 years as the public affairs/general news reporter for the *News-Star*.

Joe Worley and Lis Exon live in a "house divided." Not because of their support of opposing university football teams, but because Worley is a print journalist and Exon has worked in broadcast journalism throughout her career. Again, like all members of the Oklahoma Journalism Hall of Fame, their home is filled with awards and recognitions. Worley retired as executive editor of the *Tulsa World*, where he guided the newspaper to aggressively cover the community and state of Oklahoma. Exon has served as producer, reporter, and anchor at OETA-TV's Tulsa bureau after years of work for radio and TV stations in Orlando, Florida and Houston, Texas and national networks. Worley served as president of the Oklahoma Press Association from 2004-2005.

Finally, writing about John and Joy "Tinker" Hruby, the twelfth Hall of Fame couple, is difficult, but an honor. The Hruby family lived in Duncan and was in newspaper publishing spanning three generations. John and Tinker met while attending Schreiner University and married in Tinker's hometown of Kerrville, Texas in 1989. John became publisher of the *Duncan Banner* in 1997 and then *The Marlow Review* in 2007. According to their obituary, both worked hard to produce a quality paper for the community. John was active in the Oklahoma Press Association and both loved the Duncan community. Tinker had a passion for real estate. John had interests including ham radios and model airplanes.

John, Tinker, and their daughter Katherine were murdered in their home in October 2014. Just before his death, John had returned home from a meeting to help the Boy Scouts.

The following are the couples and the year of induction in parentheses after their names. They are listed in order of appearance in this story: Billie Rodely (2004) and Jim Palmer (2005); Poe B. Vandament (1990) and May Vandament (1990); J. Leland Gourley (1980) and Vicki Clark Gourley (2006); Alfred W. McLaughlin (1988) and Joan E. Gilmore (1994); John D. Montgomery (2005) and Gracie Montgomery (2007); Michael R. "Mick" Hinton (2003) and Sue Brewster Hinton (2009); Bill Walter (2008) and Barbara Walter (2008); Gloria Trotter (2009) and Wayne Trotter (2009); John M. Wylie II (2012) and Faith L. Wylie (2012); Joe Worley (2007) and Lis Exon (2017); and John Hruby and Joy "Tinker" Hruby (2015).

John and Tinker Hruby.

Gracie Montgomery.

John D. Montgomery.

Wayne and Gloria Trotter.

Hall of Fame couples, from left, Joan Gilmore and Al McLaughlin, Vicki Clark Gourley and J. Leland Gourley, and Billie Rodely and Jim Palmer.

JOAN GILMORE AND AL MCLAUGHLIN
picture this Hall of Fame couple
By Billie Rodely, 2004 Inductee

Joan Gilmore met Al McLaughlin while they both worked at *The Daily Oklahoman*.

McLaughlin photographed everything from prison riots to presidents. Gilmore was the Women's News Editor. They both lived Hall of Fame careers. He was inducted in 1988, and she followed in 1994.

Gilmore knew little about photography and admitted it to me, "I didn't even know how to lay out a page … he taught me a lot," including, she said, "to like fried okra in the OPUBCO cafeteria." McLaughlin worked closely with Gilmore, and together they traveled the world covering high fashion to food.

The Oklahoma City home that they shared is filled with art and journalistic history. Every wall features paintings or remembrances of the past.

Al McLaughlin (left) on November 28, 1958. Credit: Journal-Star Printing Co.

At least three Oklahoma Journalism Hall of Fame members are in this historical photo. George F. Tapscott and Bob Albright stand next to each other on the back row, far left; Al McLaughlin stands on the far right. Photo courtesy of *The Oklahoman*.

There are his awards and photos. There are her awards and photos. There are photos of the couple with presidents such as Ronald Reagan and celebrities such as Tom Selleck.

After McLaughlin's death in 2013, Gilmore continued to work as a columnist for *The Journal Record*.

When they were married in 1994, according to McLaughlin's obituary, "He didn't know (nor did she) that he would have to get permission from publisher E.K. [Edward King] Gaylord, who'd never had two department heads want to marry."

Permission was granted.

Joe Hight contributed to this essay.

Women in Communications Inc. members Joan Gilmore, Joanne Orr, and Ann Adams, from left, watch Betsy Miller demonstrate an electronic page make-up system at *The Oklahoman*. Photo by Doug Hoke. April 9, 1985. Courtesy of the Oklahoma Historical Society.

J. LELAND GOURLEY AND VICKI CLARK GOURLEY
a ring instead of a raise
By Billie Rodely, 2004 Inductee

When J. Leland Gourley rolled the presses for a new weekly Oklahoma City suburban newspaper, *FRIDAY*, in 1974, Nichols Hills was the focus of most of the content.

The circulation quickly grew, and *FRIDAY* became the largest paid circulation weekly in Oklahoma and sold advertising in The Village, Nichols Hills, and northwest Oklahoma City.

Vicki Clark Gourley's father, Stan Alexander, was mayor of The Village at that time.

As she now tells it, *FRIDAY* was long on Nichols Hills news and short on news of The Village and of her dad, the mayor. But *FRIDAY* happily accepted paid advertising from businesses in The Village. Stan Alexander's daughter was less than pleased and expressed that in a letter to Mr. J. Leland Gourley.

Vicki got a call from Leland to come into the newspaper office. He hired her in 1974 and asked her to cover The Village for the paper.

She agreed.

In a matter of a few months she was made news editor, then managing editor. Her writing and photography skills caught the attention of other organizations and, in 1976, Vicki was being courted by other papers.

So, she went into Leland's office and told him about the job offers for more money.

She would stay at the *FRIDAY*, if she got a raise.

Leland said, "How about marriage instead of a raise?"

She said, "Yes."

They said, "I do."

And, this time, the ink went on a marriage license.

JOHN AND FAITH WYLIE
Hall of Fame love from the first time they met
By Billie Rodely, 2004 Inductee

John Wylie and Faith Lubben Wylie went to separate high schools 12 miles apart in Kansas. They saw each other for the first time in an odd encounter in a yearbook office on April 6, 1971.

After doing an "undercover" educational assignment at Shawnee Mission High School, John, the yearbook editor at the all-boys Pembroke-Country Day School, decided to meet his counterpart.

"The sparks were so evident that the next morning her closest friend admitted [Faith Lubben] was working with others on a book, 'Love Story in Room 102,'" John wrote.

"Faith and I have been a committed couple ever since."

Despite being separated by colleges 600 miles apart for four years and a fifth year by 75 miles, they continued that commitment.

"We relied on seven-cent airmail stamps and letters, and one 20-minute phone call a week at operator-assisted rates of something like 30 cents a minute in 1971 dollars," he wrote. "I knew it was permanent when Faith asked me to type my letters because, as she so sweetly put it, 'I can read and savor every word.' Translation, verified by every administrative assistant and researcher I've ever had: your handwriting is utterly illegible."

In June 1976, they were married in a ceremony in which they edited their wedding vows to remove what they considered anti-feminist language. However, unlike other married couples, John and Faith celebrate their "real anniversary" on the day they met in 1971.

In April 2012, 41 years later, the Wylies were both scheduled for induction into the Oklahoma Journalism Hall of Fame. But John couldn't attend the ceremony because he was in a Tulsa hospital's intensive care unit. Their son James accepted the award for his father.

John recovered, and both Wylies are still active in journalism and

John and Faith Wylie.

writing. However, in the spring of 2019, they were in the news when their Lake Oologah home was struck by lightning and destroyed by fire. They lost thousands of journalistic documents and irreplaceable memorabilia.

Both have remained optimistic, however, as John writes: "We hope we're back in our real house by April 6, 2021, which will be our first '50th' anniversary."

Joe Hight contributed to this story.

PAMELA RUTH HENRY
disability didn't stop an extraordinary person's career
By Don Sherry

Pamela Ruth Henry's life was nothing short of extraordinary. Those of us privileged to know and work with her found our own lives enriched and challenged to do better by her indefatigable cheerfulness and her commitment to journalism. She was a trailblazer as a woman in broadcast journalism and a tireless advocate for those with disabilities. She was a poster child: an inspiration to an entire generation.

Henry was born in Ardmore, Oklahoma, in 1950. Only 14 months after her birth, she contracted polio—then an epidemic in the United States. The disease would leave her unable to walk without crutches; later in life, she was confined to a wheelchair.

Never one to indulge in self-pity, Henry described a conversation she had with her mother when she was very young: "And I just said, 'Mommy, why me?' And that's when she gave to me the strength of her belief that it's not given to you as punishment, but a random thing that happens on the planet Earth. People get diseases … but there's no reason, no answer to 'why me?' … And I never asked that question again. My question was answered."

The outgoing girl would gain national fame in 1959. She was selected to be the national polio poster child for The March of Dimes. By then, Jonas Salk's polio vaccine was in wide distribution and the disease was diminishing. But, for Henry and many thousands of others, the vaccine had come too late. She would be the last child to represent polio victims in The March of Dimes annual campaign. Henry, with her mother, set off on a nationwide tour and was photographed with celebrities and people of fame. It was in that context she met two people who would inspire her to a career in journalism: Walter Cronkite and Edward R. Murrow.

She entered the University of Oklahoma with the goal of becoming a broadcast journalist. Henry was undeterred by the fact that very few women were on-air journalists in the late 1960s and 1970s.

She worked at the campus radio station and then would get her first full-time job as a reporter and anchor at KTOK-AM in Oklahoma City—in an all-male newsroom.

Henry then went into television when she was hired as a photojournalist at WKY-TV in Oklahoma City. There were no female reporters, let alone anchors, in the state.

Again, she found herself in an all-male newsroom.

Henry's professionalism, drive, and seeming disregard for her disability won over co-workers and viewers. Her work ethic and determination were legendary.

Her career culminated in the years she spent at the Oklahoma Educational Television Authority (OETA), most of them as manager of news and public affairs.

Her retirement from television was not a retirement from work. She transferred her dedication and drive to full-time activism on behalf of people with disabilities and was chair of the Oklahoma City Mayor's Committee on Disability Concerns.

Henry referred to herself as the "sidewalk queen," as she lobbied for accessibility.

In 2004, Henry was inducted into the Oklahoma Journalism Hall of Fame. Her work on behalf of Oklahoma City's disabled is memorialized in a plaque at City Hall. Her work continued until her death on September 25, 2018.

Pam Henry at the OETA studio surveys equipment that was far different from when she began her broadcast career. The 1959 March of Dimes poster girl started her career at KTOK-AM in Oklahoma City and then was hired at WKY-TV. Retiring from OETA, she dedicated her activism on behalf of people with disabilities and was chair of the Oklahoma City Mayor's Committee on Disability Concerns.

Pam Henry accepts a donation for The March of Dimes from CBS newsman Edward R. Murrow.

WALTER AND PAM
the epitome of aplomb

By Don Sherry

Walter Cronkite was laughing.

On a winter day in 1959, in the CBS studio in New York, a precocious eight-year-old girl on crutches stood before the world map that formed the backdrop for the news set.

"I know what that's for," she said, pointing to the map with one of her crutches. To Cronkite's delight, Pam Henry presented an impromptu weather forecast.

Years later, in an exchange of letters, he would congratulate Pam on pursuing a career in journalism. He remembered their encounter well, he said, noting that Pam had shown "great aplomb."

Henry would later confess that she had to look up the definition of "aplomb."

MEMBERS INDUCTED FROM 2000 TO 2009

— 2000

Roy Angel (1920-1984), sports editor of the *Shawnee News-Star* for 35 years, covered University of Oklahoma football and kid league baseball, football, and basketball, U.S. Navy veteran stationed at Pearl Harbor during the Japanese attack in 1941.

Ed Brocksmith (1941-), newsman at KRMG Radio in Tulsa, first bureau chief to organize the news operation of the Indian Nations Radio Network, director of the office of public information at Northeastern State University.

Terry M. Clark (1944-), University of Central Oklahoma Journalism Department chairman (1990-2017), news editor of the *Clarinda Herald-Journal*, worked at the *Duncan Banner* and *The Daily Oklahoman*, owner of the *Waurika News-Democrat* (1974-1986).

Robert W. Haring (1932-2019), city editor at *The Southern Illinoisan*, worked with The Associated Press in Oklahoma, Arkansas, Ohio, and New York, served as bureau chief in New Jersey, executive editor of the *Tulsa World*, established the Tulsa Literacy Coalition, Tulsa Mentoring Council, *Tulsa World* Online, Tulsa Run, and the FreeWheel bicycle ride.

Katherine Hatch (1934-2012), reporter at the *Kansas City Times*, worked at *TIME* Magazine in New York, covered the Harry S. Truman administration with United Press International, worked with *The Daily Oklahoman*, foreign correspondent for international newspapers in Mexico and Central America, author of three books.

Jim Henderson (1942-), worked with the *Elk City Daily News, Clinton Daily News,* and *Tulsa World,* named Outstanding Oklahoma Newsman by the Oklahoma State University School of Journalism, named a Nieman Fellow, reporter for the *Dallas Times Herald*, Dallas bureau chief for the *Houston Chronicle*.

Jan Lovell (1934-2014), OETA State Capitol Bureau chief, worked with KVSO and KNOR, anchor and producer at KWTV, KTVY, and KAUT, chair of the broadcast press corps at the state Capitol.

Robert H. "Bob" Peterson (1927-2004), editor of the *5th Air Force Command Report* in Japan, editor of the *Oklahoma Daily*, reporter for *The Lawton Constitution* and the *Lawton Morning Press* and the United Press International in Oklahoma City, owner-publisher of the *Durant Daily Democrat*, Oklahoma Press Association Half Century Club member.

Charles Ward (1918-1999), editor of the *Cleburne County Times*, Army veteran, editor of the *Oklahoma Daily*, editor for the *Sooner State Press*, headed the Norman bureau for *The Oklahoman* and *Oklahoma City Times*, worked with the Oklahoma Press Association, news editor of the *Poteau News*, general manager of the *Durant Daily Democrat*, administrative assistant of House Speaker Carl Albert and U.S. Senator David Boren.

— 2001

Osa Lee Banzett (1906-1977), worked with her husband, Don Banzett, on the *Edmond Booster* and the *Edmond Enterprise*, co-owner of several weekly papers in Oklahoma and Arkansas, inducted into the Edmond Historical Society's Roll of Honor.

Ida B Blackburn (1929-2016), worked as "Ida B" for the nationally syndicated *Romper Room* on KOCO-TV, Oklahoma's first Hollywood correspondent, host of *The Ida B Show*, public relations and advertising agency owner.

Milton B. Garber (1912-1994), editor and co-publisher of the *Enid Morning News* and *Enid Daily Eagle* for 40 years, military veteran, worked for *Stars and Stripes* in the Pacific, president of the Enid Rotary and Chamber of Commerce, United Press Publishers, and Oklahoma Press Association (1963).

Robert L. Haught (1930-), cartoonist for the *Thunderbird News* of the Oklahoma 45th Division, bureau manager for United Press International in Oklahoma City, press secretary for Governor and then U.S. Senator Henry Bellmon, first Washington-based editorial writer for *The Daily Oklahoman*, National Press Club member, helped create the Will Rogers Humanitarian Award for newspaper columnists.

H.C. Neal (1922-2002), served in the Army as a paratrooper in World War II and Korea, news editor at the *Watonga Republican* and the *Okemah Daily Leader*, chief of the Edmond bureau for *The Daily Oklahoman*, editor of the *Edmond Sun* and *Edmond Booster*.

Maebeth "Beth" Ray (1927-), operator at *The Lawton Constitution* and *Morning Press, Cyril News, Woodward County News, Leedey Star* and for papers at Taloga, Vici, Seiling, and Custer City, co-owner of the *Yale News*, Oklahoma Press Association Half Century Club member.

Mark Singer (1950-), staff writer for *The New Yorker* Magazine, worked with the *Tulsa Tribune*, author of several books, including *Funny Money*, featuring the Penn Square Bank collapse in Oklahoma City and statewide oil bust.

Jack D. Willis (1940-), worked at the *Muskogee Daily Phoenix* and *Times Democrat*, journalism lecturer and editorial adviser for the *Oklahoma Daily*, mentor to young journalists, including Pulitzer Prize winners.

Pendleton Woods (1923-2014), editor of the *Arkansas Traveler*, public information officer for the 45th Infantry Division during the Korean War, reporter, editor, and columnist for the *Southwest American* at Fort Smith, editor of the OG&E company magazine, established the Oklahoma Oral History program.

— **2002**

E.G. "Bob" Albright (1922-2010), photographer for *The Daily Oklahoman* and *Oklahoma City Times*, World War II veteran, twice named Photographer of the Year by the Oklahoma Press Association, featured in the Oklahoma Historical Society's 50 Years of Photojournalism exhibit.

J. Landis Fleming (1907-1997), worked with multiple Oklahoma newspapers, editor of the *Oklahoma Advisor* and *North Star, Moore Monitor, Bristow News,* and *Kingfisher Times and Free Press*, recipient of the Bill Crawford Memorial Media in the Arts Award.

Francis Langdon (1922-2003), publisher of the *Tonkawa News* for 42 years, combat submarine veteran in World War II, president of the Oklahoma Press Association (1978) and the Oklahoma Newspaper Foundation, honored with OPA's Beachy Musselman Award, founding trustee of the National Recreation and Park Association.

W.U. McCoy (1921-2012), author of *Performing and Visual Arts Writing and Reviewing*, named Outstanding Journalist at Arkansas State University, feature editor for Western News Service, editor at several Texas newspapers, worked with *The Daily Oklahoman* and *Oklahoma City Times*.

Frances "Fran" Morris (1930-), worked as "Miss Fran" every morning on KWTV from 1958 to 1967, writer for WTAR-TV and KWTV, writer, producer, and hostess of *Storyland*, advocate for children's mental health, worked at KFOR for 17 years.

Jim Myers (1947-), political and government reporter, worked for *The Enid News & Eagle* and *The Lawton Constitution*, statehouse bureau and Washington correspondent for the *Tulsa World*, Paul Miller Fellow for the Freedom Forum, Knight Center Fellow at the University of Maryland.

Pam Olson (1949-), first woman to anchor a prime-time television newscast in Oklahoma City, anchor for KWTV, wrote and produced the "Gift of Life" documentary, worked with CBS in the Atlanta bureau and with CNN as White House correspondent, freelance writer for the *Tulsa World*.

James H. Reid (1917-2005), wrote for *Stars and Stripes* during World War II, worked for the *Muskogee Daily Phoenix* as reporter, farm editor, and photographer, covered police courts, education, and business at *The Daily Oklahoman* for 31 years.

Dave Story (1930-2009), military newspaper editor at several Strategic Air Command bases, worked at newspapers in Arkansas and Alaska, editor of the *Frederick Leader* and the *Guymon Herald*, publisher of the *Claremore Daily Progress*, recipient of OPA's Milt Phillips Award and the Beachy Musselman Award.

— **2003**

David G. Averill (1945-), associate editor of the *Tulsa World*, recipient of numerous awards for his reporting on desegregation in the 1970s, editorial writer and Sunday columnist since 1985, board chairman for Tulsa Habitat for Humanity.

Bob G. Burke (1948-), lawyer, historian, author or co-author of more books on history than any other author, including nearly 135 Oklahoma historical biographies and other books preserving and celebrating Oklahoma's rich heritage, radio-television journalist and sportscaster for KBEI, color analyst for the University of Oklahoma basketball network, news director of KOMA, news editor for KTOK, announcer for ABC Sports in New York, and Oklahoma Secretary of Commerce under Governor David Boren.

Larry Hammer (1937-2001), owner of multiple Oklahoma papers, sports editor of the *Okmulgee Daily Times*, president of the Oklahoma Press Association (1976), recipient of OPA's H. Milt Phillips Award, awarded an honorary Master's of Laws degree from Northwestern Oklahoma State University.

James L. "Jim" Hartz (1940-), news anchor at KOME, KRMG, KOTV, KNBC-TV, PBS-TV, and WRC-TV, co-anchored the *Today Show* with Barbara Walters, military and aerospace reporter for NBC News, correspondent in the Yom Kippur War, winner of five Emmy awards.

Michael R. "Mick" Hinton (1944-), final city editor for the *Oklahoma City Times*, worked with *The Daily Oklahoman*, *Norman Transcript,* and *Lawton Morning Press*, president of the Oklahoma City Society of Professional Journalists chapter.

Suzanne A. Holloway (1914-2018), restaurant critic for the *Tulsa World*, wrote the "Chef's Choice" column for 24 years, second woman to serve as editor of the University of Oklahoma *Oklahoma Daily*, worked with *The Daily Oklahoman*.

Carl "Ed" Kelley (1953-), worked with *The Daily Oklahoman* as editor and Washington bureau chief, named editor of the year by the National Press Foundation for coverage of the 1995 Oklahoma City bombing, business and city editor for OPUBCO, worked on the University of Oklahoma *Oklahoma Daily*, Pulitzer Prize juror, dean of the Gaylord College of Journalism & Mass Communication.

Rebecca "Becky" Mayo (1941-), educational services director of the *Sequoyah County Times*, co-winner of the Oklahoma Press Association's Beachy Musselman Award, pioneered a comprehensive Newspaper in Education program, first chairperson of the Oklahoma Newspaper Foundation Committee on Newspapers in Education.

Anthony "Tony" Pippen (1936-), business editor for the *Ada Evening News*, editor of the *Harding College Bison*, editor for multiple Missouri newspapers, president of The Associated Press in Oklahoma, original member of the American Publishing Managing Editor's board in three states.

— 2004

Darrell Barton (1942-2015), chief photographer at WKY/KTVY Channel 4 in Oklahoma City, longtime National Press Photographers Association member, TV news photographer at KAKW-TV, twice named photographer of the year by NPPA, featured on *48 Hours* on CBS.

Phil E. Brown (1927-2009), feature writer, columnist, city editor, managing editor, and news editor for the *Enid News & Eagle*, wrote news for KCRC Radio for 25 years, member of the Oklahoma Press Association's Half-Century Club, charter member of the Enid Sunrise Lions.

Pam Henry (1950-2018), first female reporter and first woman anchor for KTOK in Oklahoma City, producer, public affairs program host, and capitol reporter for WKY-TV, worked with KOCO-TV and KSWO, served OETA as an expert in election coverage.

Jack Lancaster (1950-2013), sports editor at his hometown *Alva Review-Courier*, sports editor and managing editor for the *Elk City News*, news adviser of *The Daily O'Collegian* at Oklahoma State University, recipient of the Oklahoma Press Association Beachy Musselman Award.

Rusty Danenhour Lang (1947-), student editor of the newspaper at East Central University in Ada, award-winning reporter at the *Daily Ardmoreite*, general assignment reporter, U.C. Living Section editor and medical reporter for the *Tulsa World*, Okemah Hall of Fame honoree.

Edward K. Livermore, Jr. (1944-), worked with United Press International, the *Claremore Progress*, *Sapulpa Herald, Grand Junction Sentinel*, and *Altus Times Democrat*, editor of the *Edmond Sun* and the University of Oklahoma *Oklahoma Daily*, owner of the *Mineral Wells Index* and the *Guthrie News Leader*, Oklahoma Press Association president (1993), Edmond Citizen of the Year, Edmond Hall of Fame inductee.

Fred W. Marvel (1943-), photographer for the Oklahoma Department of Tourism and Recreation, served in the U.S. Army, active member of the National Press Photographers Association, photo-historian for the Oklahoma Historical Society.

William "Bill" May (1938-), attended the Navy Journalism School, worked for *the Fort Worth Star-Telegram*, the *Arlington Citizen-Journal* (Texas), the *Duncan Banner*, *The Daily Oklahoman, Oklahoma City Times, The Journal Record*, and KTOK, president of the Moore Optimist Club.

Billie Rodely (1953-), worked with WIOU Radio in Kokomo, Indiana, KFKF Radio in Kansas City, Missouri, and KTOK and WKY radio in Oklahoma City, radio news anchor, editor, and reporter at Clear Channel Communications, worked with the OETA TV production department, serves on the Executive Committee for the Oklahoma Journalism Hall of Fame.

— 2005

David G. Fitzgerald (1935-), worked with combat photographer George Tapscott in the 45th Division of the National Guard, published at least 10 photography books, major contributor to *Oklahoma Today*, three-time Photographer of the Year, documentarian of human crises, including the 2004 tsunami in Indonesia.

Dr. Haskell O. "Woody" Gaddis (1935-2008), established the photography program at the University of Central Oklahoma, staff photographer at the *Tulsa Daily World*, photographer and instructor at Central State University, served on numerous community and college committees.

Sue Lewis Hale (1944-), leading First Amendment advocate, reporter for the *Oklahoma City Times*, editor of the *EI Reno Tribune*, executive editor for *The Oklahoman*, founding member and president of Freedom of Information Oklahoma, president of the National Freedom of Information Coalition, president of Oklahoma's Society of Professional Journalists and Associated Press/Oklahoma News Executives.

Bettye Jane Johnston (1921-2014), journalism and photography teacher at Bartlesville is Sooner High School, columnist for the *Pawhuska Journal-Capital*, editor of the Northern Oklahoma College *Maverick* and Central State University's *The Vista*, taught journalism at Central State University, freelance writer for the *Bartlesville Examiner-Enterprise*.

James A. Killackey (1948-2018), worked with the *Tulsa Tribune*, managing editor of the *Oklahoma Daily*, reporter for *The Daily Oklahoman*, Ford Foundation fellow, president of the National Education Writers Association, Association of Health Care Journalists member, president of the University of Oklahoma Journalism Alumni Board.

Mike McCormick (1948-), city, managing, and executive editor of the *Shawnee News-Star*, award-winning editorial writer, served on the board of St. Gregory's University, president of the Oklahoma Press/Oklahoma News Executives.

John D. Montgomery (1954-), worked with the *Hobart Daily Democrat-Chief, Kiowa County Star Review, The Daily Oklahoman, Oklahoma City Times, Tulsa World* and the *Madill Record*, co-owner of the *Purcell Register*, president of the Oklahoma Press Association, board member and Oklahoma State chairman of the National Newspaper Association.

James G. Palmer (1943-), anchor, reporter, and news director at many Oklahoma City radio stations, including WKY, KOMA-AM, KMGL-FM, and KTOK, worked at WRIT in Milwaukee, Wisconsin, KDNT in Denton, Texas, KADS in Elk City, and KWCO in Chickasha, regional broadcast executive with United Press International in Dallas, Texas, worked with Fox Channel 25 in Oklahoma City.

Dave Sittler (1945-), sportswriter for the *Lincoln Journal Star, The Daily Oklahoman, Tulsa Tribune, Omaha World Herald,* and *Tulsa World*, named Sportswriter of the Year for Oklahoma five times by the National Sportscasters and Sportswriters Association, president of the Football Writers Association of America.

Terri Watkins (1954-), worked with KAKS, KNOR, KLUF, KOCY, KTOK, KOCO-TV, and OETA, two-time recipient of the Peabody Award, hosted ABC's *Nightline* during the Denver trial of Timothy McVeigh, president of Freedom of Information Oklahoma.

— **2006**

Jerry Bohnen (1948-), news director of KTOK Radio, Oklahoma News Network, and Clear Channel Communications, worked with KMAN, KWBW, and the *Wichita Eagle*, founder and president of the Association of News Broadcasters of Kansas, recipient of the Investigative Reporter and Editors Award and The Edward R. Murrow Award.

Jennifer Duffy Gilliland (1952-), worked with the Oklahoma Press Association and *The Oklahoman*, editor of *The Oklahoma Publisher*, writer and designer at Oklahoma County Newspapers, president of Freedom of Information Oklahoma, Oklahoma Journalism Hall of Fame Executive Committee member.

Vicki Clark Gourley (1946-), chairman of Nichols Hills Publishing Company, executive editor of *FRIDAY* newspaper, featured photographer in *National Geographic's* "Crossing America" and on Publisher's Auxiliary's cover, recipient of the National Conference of Christian and Jews Humanitarian Award and the JCPenney Golden Rule Award.

Jenk Jones, Jr. (1936-), worked with the *Tulsa Tribune, Colorado Daily, Minneapolis Tribune,* and the *Anchorage Times,* treasurer and director of the Associated Press Managing Editors' Association, journalism and political history professor, recipient of The Nature Conservancy's Conservation Award.

Jim Langdon (1950-), associate publisher for *The Tonkawa News,* managed the Oklahoma Press Association's Oklahoma Newspaper Advertising Bureau, president of American Newspaper Representatives, founder of Langdon Publishing Company, established *Tulsa People Magazine,* recipient of the Distinguished Alumni Award from the University of Oklahoma School of Journalism.

Danna Sue Walker (1941-), society editor and columnist for the *Tulsa World,* inducted into The University of Tulsa Communications Hall of Fame, recipient of the Bill Crawford Memorial Award for her commitment to the arts.

George R. Wilson (1941-), photo editor of his high school yearbook and newspaper, photographer for Pipkin Photo, chief photographer of the *Oklahoma Journal,* director of photography for *The Daily Oklahoman* and the *Oklahoma City Times.*

Fritz W. Wirt (1935-), worked with the *Clinton Daily News, The Daily Oklahoman, Kingsport Times-News, Temple Daily Telegram, EI Paso Times, San Angelo Standard Times, Del Rio News-Herald, Huntsville Item,* and *Harte-Hanks,* general manager of Oklahoma State University's *The O'Collegian.*

John V. Young (1934-), sports editor of the *Cushing Daily Citizen,* worked with United Press International in Dallas, Texas and Kansas City, Missouri, editor of the *Sapulpa Daily Herald,* news editor for the *Tulsa Tribune,* assistant news editor at the *Tulsa World,* recipient of the Oklahoma Press Association's Beachy Musselman Award.

— **2007**

David Dary (1934-2018), journalist in Kansas, Texas, and Washington, D.C. with CBS News and NBC News, journalism professor at the University of Kansas for 20 years, head of what is now the University of Oklahoma Gaylord College of Journalism, author of 20 books on the American West, including a history of the Oklahoma Publishing Company and the Gaylord family.

Gracie Montgomery (1956-), co-publisher of *The Purcell Register*, served as the third female Oklahoma Press Association president, worked with the *Johnston County Capital-Democrat*, appointed by Supreme Court Chief Justice Marian P. Opala to the original Oklahoma Ethics Commission.

Patrick O'Dell (1938-), staff cameraman at the CBS Southwest Bureau in Dallas, Texas, news director at KOTV in Tulsa, worked with WSB-TV in Atlanta, Georgia, filmed Dr. Martin Luther King, Jr. and other Civil Rights leaders, won an Emmy for coverage of the 1985 Mexico City earthquake.

Phillip Parrish (1937-), named national wrestling sportswriter of the year, sports editor of the *Norman Transcript* and *Lawton Morning Press*, editor of the *Tulsa County News*, executive sports editor at the *Tulsa World*, received a Lifetime Achievement Award from the Oklahoma Professional Chapter of the Society of Professional Journalists.

Bob Sands (1950-), worked with OETA and numerous other stations, chief investigator for NBC's *Nightly News* on the Oklahoma City bombing, worked for ABC News *Primetime*, CNN, and NBC *Dateline*, received a Lifetime Achievement Award from the Oklahoma Professional Chapter of the Society of Professional Journalists, board member of Freedom of Information Oklahoma, president of the Oklahoma Associated Press Broadcasters and the Oklahoma City News Broadcasters Association.

Mike Shannon (1948-), longtime managing editor of *The Oklahoman*, worked for the *Oklahoma Daily*, worked with the *Oklahoma City Times* as reporter, assistant editor, city editor, executive news editor, and assistant managing editor.

Mike Sowell (1948-), reporter and editor of the U.S. Army's *The Berlin Observer*, sportswriter and assistant sports editor at *The El Paso Times*, sports columnist and editor for the *Tulsa Tribune*, winner of the Associated Press Sports Editors national column writing contest, author of two *New York Times* Notable Books of the Year.

Mark Thomas (1959-), executive vice president and secretary of the Oklahoma Press Association, assistant manager of the Oklahoma Newspaper Advertising Bureau, worked with the *Edmond Sun*, executive director of the Colorado Press Association, president of Freedom of Information Oklahoma, president of the Newspaper Association Managers.

Helen Ford Wallace (1940-), columnist for *The Oklahoman* for more than 50 years, wrote for the *Oklahoma Daily*, taught journalism at Northeast High School, served as chairman and president of several organizations, including the Beaux Arts Ball, the Oklahoma City Junior League, and the University of Oklahoma Mother's Club.

Joe Worley (1947-), executive editor of the *Tulsa World*, city editor, managing editor, and executive editor at the *Nashville Banner*, news director at the University of Tennessee, president of the Oklahoma Press Association, American Society of News Editors and Associated Press/ Oklahoma News Executive member, served in the Tennessee and Oklahoma Army National Guard.

— 2008

William P. Bleakley (1943-), night editor and columnist for *The Guam Daily News* while serving in the Navy, co-founder of the MAPS for Kids project, founder of *The Oklahoma Gazette*, formed the Tierra Media Group, which includes magazine, online, and wireless publishing.

Gerry Bonds (1944-), news anchor at WTNH-TV in Connecticut, prime time news anchor at KOCO-TV for nine years, co-anchor of the nightly *Oklahoma News Report* with OETA, hosted the weekly Oklahoma City Metro program, which earned an Emmy award and two nominations, recipient of the 2006 Governor's Arts Award for media.

Ann DeFrange (1943-2012), worked with *The Oklahoman* and *Oklahoma City Times* as reporter, copy editor, layout editor, manager, head of the Women's News department, and creator of the Life and Leisure section, contributing founder and director of the award-winning Newsroom 101 program for high school students.

Donna Barron Evers (1946-), director of public relations for the *Pauls Valley Daily Democrat*, reporter and editor for *The Lawton Constitution*, newspaper adviser of *The Collegian* at Cameron University, where she was Professor of the Year in 1993.

Bill Harper (1943-), sports news desk editor, administrative sports editor, and columnist for the *Tulsa Tribune*, operations editor for the *Tulsa World*, recipient of awards from The Associated Press, Oklahoma Coaches Association, and Oklahoma National Guard, conducted several layout and design workshops in the region.

Lindel G. Hutson (1946-), reporter and editor for The Associated Press in Little Rock, Arkansas, Associated Press news editor in Indiana, Associated Press Oklahoma Chief of Bureau, worked with the *Jonesboro Sun* in Arkansas and the *Texarkana Gazette*, worked as a United States Army journalist in the U.S. and with NATO in Europe, contributing founder and president of Freedom of Information Oklahoma, served on the Executive Committee for the Oklahoma Journalism Hall of Fame.

Paul B. Southerland (1956-), worked for *The Oklahoman*, *Oklahoma Daily*, and *Oklahoma City Times*, Newspaper Photographer of the Year, winner of more than 100 photo and reporting awards, officer in the Oklahoma News Photographers Association, 32-year member of the National Press Photographers Association.

Barbara A. Walter (1944-), teen correspondent for the *Oklahoma City Times* at Classen High School, editor of the Oklahoma Press Association's *Publisher*, managing editor and co-publisher of *The Hennessey Clipper*, Oklahoma Press Association president (2002), first female president of the Oklahoma Newspaper Foundation.

Bill Walter (1935-2017), editor, publisher, and third-generation owner of *The Hennessey Clipper*, worked at the *Oklahoma Daily, Alva Review-Courier,* and Oklahoma Baptist University *Press*, public relations practitioner, served on Oklahoma Press Association committees.

— **2009**

Sharon K. Dowell (1947-), longest-serving food editor in *The Oklahoman's* history, worked at the *Perry Daily Chief* (Iowa) and the *Daily Law Journal Record* in Oklahoma City, writer for World Neighbors, the Oklahoma Water Resources Board, and the State Fair of Oklahoma, longtime member of the National Association of Food Editors.

Lewis Ferguson (1934-2017), sports and wire editor of *The Ponca City News*, sports announcer for WBBZ, worked with the Associated Press in Oklahoma City, Sioux Falls, South Dakota, Minneapolis, Minnesota, and Kansas City, Missouri, correspondent for the Associated Press Topeka Statehouse bureau, recipient of the University of Oklahoma Journalism Distinguished Alumnus Award.

Sue Brewster Hinton (1949-), Oklahoma City Community College (OCCC) journalism professor and faculty adviser of *The Pioneer*, first recipient of OCCC's President's Award for Excellence in Teaching, named Outstanding Journalism Educator in 1994 by Women in Communications, Inc., worked for *The Oklahoman, Norman Transcript*, and *Lawton Morning Press.*

Debbie Jackson (1949-), longtime Sunday editor for the *Tulsa World*, editor of the *Henryetta Daily Free-Lance*, assistant news editor of *The Oklahoma Journal*, lead editor on all *Tulsa World* special sections, organized and produced coverage of three Centennial celebrations—Tulsa's, the World's, and Oklahoma's—including three books.

Russell M. Perry (1939-), founder of *The Black Chronicle*, co-publisher of *The Black Dispatch*, president of Perry Publishing & Broadcasting, Commerce Secretary in the Frank Keating administration, Federal Reserve Bank of Kansas City advisory committee member, inducted into the Oklahoma City Public Schools Foundation Wall of Fame.

Dick Pryor (1955-), Emmy award-winning journalist, deputy director of OETA, anchor of the *Oklahoma News Report* for more than 17 years, sports director of KNOR Radio in Norman and KFDX-TV in Wichita Falls, Texas, sports anchor and reporter at KJRH-TV in Tulsa and KOCO-TV in Oklahoma City.

Ray Soldan (1929-), covered more than 1,000 football games for *The Oklahoman*, sports editor of the *Daily Kansan*, worked at the *Beatrice Daily Sun* (Nebraska), sports editor at the *Lawton Morning Press*, named Oklahoma Sportswriter of the Year, Oklahoma Sports Hall of Fame and Oklahoma Basketball Coaches Hall of Fame inductee.

Gloria Trotter (1944-), co-publisher of the *Tecumseh Countywide News* and *The Shawnee Sun*, combined into *The Countywide & Sun*, worked on the Bristol Virginia-Tennessean, worked with WCYB-TV and WOPI, president of the Oklahoma Press Association (2009) and of Freedom of Information Oklahoma, recipient of the National Newspaper Association's McKinney Award and the Outstanding Journalism Alumni Award from Memphis State University.

Wayne Trotter (1939-), co-publisher of the *Tecumseh Countywide News* and *The Shawnee Sun*, combined into *The Countywide & Sun*, worked at multiple newspapers, two-time winner of best editorial in the National Newspaper Association contest, recipient of the Oklahoma Press Association's Beachy Musselman and Milt Phillips awards, Oklahoma Press Association president (1999).

THE 2010 - 2019 DECADE

family dynasties, broadcast pioneers, northeast Oklahomans, and changes in the Hall of Fame

The fifth decade of the Oklahoma Journalism Hall of Fame kicked off with dynasties and broadcast pioneers.

Three more Dyers were added during the decade. Brothers and community publishers Ray and Sean Dyer were both inducted in 2010. Kelly Dyer Fry, who became publisher of *The Oklahoman*, became the sixth family member to join the Hall of Fame in 2014.

Also, in 2010, Mike Boettcher became a member. Boettcher's distinguished career included being the first to do a live satellite report for the launch of a "fledgling" cable TV network: CNN. Dr. Paul Lehman, who was the first African-American news person in the Oklahoma City market in 1968, was inducted in 2017. George Tomek, a Navy Reserve captain, was part of WKY-TV in the 1960s and joined the Hall of Fame in 2018. And master storyteller Bob Dotson completed his four million miles before being inducted in 2019.

Five late journalists, one famed for international reporting, one known for his work in Oklahoma, and three community publishers were inducted during the decade. Jim Standard, a former executive editor of *The Oklahoman* who later became a preacher, was inducted in 2011, a year after his death. Anthony Shadid, the famed two-time Pulitzer Prize winner, was inducted the same year that he died in 2012. And third-generation publisher Ray Lokey was told just days before his death in 2017 that he would be part of the 2018 induction class. The three joined John A. and Joy "Tinker" Hruby, co-publishers of the *Marlow Review* and co-owner of the *Comanche County Chronicle*, who were inducted in 2015 after they were killed in their home the previous year.

Also, in 2020, the posthumous award of membership was awarded to ten journalists only for the second time in the Hall of Fame's history.

Northeast Oklahoma was well-represented during the decade. Susan Ellerbach, later executive editor of the *Tulsa World*, became a member in 2010. Investigative reporter Mary Hargrove, who was nominated by Pulitzer finalist Ziva Branstetter, was inducted in 2018. Branstetter was inducted in 2019. John M. II and Faith Wylie were both inducted in 2012. Besides being co-publisher with his wife, John Wylie was also known for being part of the *Kansas City Star* team that won the Pulitzer for coverage of the Hyatt disaster in 1982. And, noted community journalist Ralph Schaefer became a member in 2017, 16 years after being first nominated.

Video tributes replaced the sometimes long speeches for the first time in 2017. They were instituted by Joe Hight, who was inducted in 2013. Hight became the first Hall of Fame member to take over as director after he was inducted. His induction was a year before he was editor of Colorado Springs *Gazette*, which won the Pulitzer Prize in National Reporting for Dave Philipps' "Other than Honorable" project. The 50th anniversary celebration included a redesigned website, a coffee-table book, a documentary, and the opening of a small museum and other improvements. The year before, Hight worked with student coordinators Erin Barnett and Trevor Stone to organize a First Amendment Day at the University of Central Oklahoma as part of the induction day ceremonies.

Brian Blansett completes notes during a break in the action between the Meeker vs. Luther high school football game. Blansett covered sporting events for Meeker, McLoud, Dale, North Rock Creek, and some of Stroud. He knew almost everyone in the bleachers for Meeker and people would say hello and chat. Photo courtesy of Kindra Coffman.

Dr. Paul Lehman (right) along with Dr. Stan Hoig, featured speakers at a symposium titled "The Oklahoma Past: Land, People and Politics." Discussions focused on how Oklahomans were viewed.

Finally, the Goodwin family dynasty continued in 2015 when brothers Edward "Ed" Goodwin, Jr. and James O. Goodwin followed their father, E.L. Goodwin, into the Hall of Fame. Ed Goodwin's biography noted that he was "born with a torch in his hand and heart" that propelled him to follow the family legacy of being active in the civil rights movement. Robert "Bob" Goodwin, joined them as a Lifetime Achievement Award recipient in 2020.

Steve Booher, right, retired after 34 years as general manager and publisher of the *Cherokee Messenger & Republican*. Rusty Ferguson is pictured on the left.

Vice President Dan Quayle makes a point during an editorial board meeting at *The Oklahoman* with Oklahoma Journalism Hall of Fame members, from left, Jim Standard, Jim Lange, Pat McGuigan, and Deacon New. Longtime editorial writer Leonard Jackson, right, was also at the meeting.

The *Tulsa World's* Wayne Greene working as an election official at the University Club Towers polling place in Tulsa, Oklahoma. June 26, 2018. Photo by Stephen Pingry. Courtesy of the *Tulsa World*.

Allan Cromley, longtime Washington Bureau chief for *The Daily Oklahoman* and *Oklahoma City Times*, asks a question of President Ronald Reagan at *The Oklahoman's* offices. Edward L. Gaylord, left, and Jim Standard were also in the room along with an unidentified stenographer. Cromley, Gaylord, and Standard are all Hall of Fame members. Photo courtesy of *The Oklahoman*.

James Watts looks over the Jason Lee photo exhibit at Tulsa's Philbrook Museum of Art on May 30, 2019. Photo by Tom Gilbert. Courtesy of the *Tulsa World.*

Tulsa Press Club, for *Tulsa World* newsletter: from left to right are Janet Pearson, David Averill, and Susan Holloway. April 22, 2003. Photo by Robert S. Cross. Courtesy of the *Tulsa World*.

Julie DelCour with The University of Tulsa President J. Paschal Twyman in 1980. Photo by Brandi Stafford. Courtesy of the *Tulsa World*.

Then presidential candidate Barack Obama talks with *Tulsa World* reporter Randy Krehbiel and his son Jay Krehbiel during Obama's stop at the Educare Center in Tulsa, Oklahoma. March 19, 2007. Photo by Michael Wyke. Courtesy of the *Tulsa World*.

Robert W. Portiss (left), port director of the Tulsa Port of Catoosa, greets *Tulsa World's* Mike Jones, and others with the *World's* editorial board, in the port's administrative building in Catoosa. December 3, 2014. Photo by Cory Young. Courtesy of the *Tulsa World*.

Susan and Mary Ellerbach work on the computer in Susan's office. Photo by Kelly Kerr. Courtesy of the *Tulsa World*.

Susan Ellerbach, pictured in the *Tulsa World* newsroom, became executive editor in November of 2014. Courtesy of the *Tulsa World*.

Susan Ellerbach talks with Melani Hamilton and Abby Lehman in the *Tulsa World* newsroom. This is a set up photo. Photo by Mike Simons. Courtesy of the *Tulsa World*.

Oklahoma City's 26-story Biltmore Hotel, built in 1932, was demolished to make way for an urban renewal project, The Myriad Botanical Gardens. At the time it was the tallest steel-reinforced building in the world ever demolished with explosives. It required 991 separate explosive charges in the building to bring it down. Photo by Paul B. Southerland. October 16, 1977.

City photographer Doug Hoke didn't need a flashbulb for this night picture, getting a nice assist from lightning flashing over the campus of Central State University in Edmond. 1976. *Oklahoma Times*. Courtesy of the Oklahoma Historical Society.

Doug Hoke snapped this picture of a miniature Uncle Sam providing extra pedal power to Central State's Homecoming parade in October. 1975. Courtesy of the Oklahoma Historical Society.

Whiticker, pensive feline that he is, peers into the camera's semi-fisheye adapter, amazed at the sophistication of modern photographic equipment. 1976. *Oklahoma Times*. Doug Hoke photo. Courtesy of the Oklahoma Historical Society.

89ers catcher Doug Davis tags out New Orleans' Dave Nilsson at the plate during the first inning of Thursday's game. June 10, 1993. *The Daily Oklahoman*. Doug Hoke photo. Courtesy of the Oklahoma Historical Society.

Byron Houston had been a towering presence for Oklahoma State University. February 15, 1990. *The Daily Oklahoman*. Doug Hoke photo. Courtesy of the Oklahoma Historical Society.

Miss America Susan Powell of Elk City, Oklahoma in a recording studio in Oklahoma City, concentrating on the music to "Oklahoma." Photo by Paul B. Southerland. March 18, 1981.

THE GOODWIN FAMILY LEGACY
time to celebrate, appreciate, and reflect on the Eagle
By David Goodwin

In 2003, I was named editor of *The Middletown Journal* in Ohio. It was an occasion to celebrate, to appreciate, and to reflect.

Celebrate: I was a rarity in daily newspaper leadership. I was one of only 11 African-American journalists as an editor at one of the more than 1,450 daily newspapers in the United States in 2003.

Appreciate: I was not a rarity within my family, however. I was merely following my family's vocation. I am a fourth-generation journalist. My paternal great-grandfather, James Henri Goodwin, who had a fourth-grade education, was named business manager of *The Tulsa Star* in 1916 by publisher and editor A.J. Smitherman, the first African-American newspaper editor and publisher to produce a long-running daily in the state of Oklahoma. My maternal great-grandfather, James Ballard Osby, started a fledging newspaper in Springfield, Illinois. From their lineage came journalists who became pioneers integrating newspapers in Tulsa, Oklahoma; Flint, Michigan; Kansas City, Missouri; Indianapolis, Indiana; as well as an editor of the *Louisiana Weekly* and a contributor to the NAACP's *The Crisis* Magazine.

Most notably, I followed the path of Edward Lawrence Goodwin, Sr., an inductee in 1980, who purchased *The Oklahoma Eagle* in 1936 because he was tired of being vilified by the Tulsa metropolitan press that disparagingly labeled him as "the black mayor of the City of Tulsa ... because of the fact that I had become involved in all of these illegal operations. ... So, the metropolitan press was so strong in their accusations against me, I said, 'Well, I guess this is a good thing for me to do. I'm going to buy one of these papers.'"

Instead of trying to restore and reshape his reputation, my grandfather discovered that his mission was far more consequential. "... I decided that I would dedicate the rest of my life fighting for the things that I knew that black people needed and never had in order to elevate them to a higher social level, a higher economic level, than that they'd been accustomed to." He stamped this mission below the masthead, "We Make America Great When We Aid Our People."

My grandfather served as editor and publisher for four decades, and earned national respect with his lifelong campaign for civil and human rights. Today, *The Eagle* remains the lone black-owned business still in operation since the heydays of Greenwood's famous "Black Wall Street of America."

My grandfather mentored scores of journalists who became trailblazers in their own rights. Among those individuals were:

- *Eagle* editor Edgar T. Rouzeau worked at the *New York Herald Tribune* and was the first African American to be accredited to cover World War II.

- Editor Thelma Thurston Gorham wrote a national award-winning series of front-page editorials in 1954-55 on integration, using the theme, "Are We Ready?" She would later serve as executive editor of the *The Black Dispatch* in Oklahoma City, a reporter for *Ebony* and *Jet* magazines, and a journalism professor and dean at four universities.

- Luix Virgil Overbea, who served stints both as city editor and sports editor, became one of the first blacks to integrate a Southern newspaper, the *Winston-Salem Journal and Sentinel* in North Carolina. He later worked for the *St. Louis Sentinel,* the *St. Louis Globe-Democrat,* and the *Christian Science Monitor.*

- Editorial editor and columnist Benjamin Hill served from 1951-1971 and was one of Tulsa's leading religious figures and a state lawmaker.

- Staff writer Carmen Fields was a member of *The Boston Globe's* team that was awarded the Pulitzer Prize for its massive and balanced coverage of the Boston school desegregation crisis and later became the first African American to hold a newsroom leadership position. She later worked as a reporter and anchor for WHDH-TV and WGBH-TV in Boston, Massachusetts.

- Editor and columnist Don Ross later worked as a columnist and assistant managing editor at the *Post-Tribune* in Gary, Indiana. He was a celebrated writer who formed an alliance with syndicated columnists Art Buckwald, Russell Baker, Erma Bombeck, and Andy Rooney to create an unofficial club, the "Academy of Humor Columnists." As an Oklahoma legislator, Ross sponsored the bill that created the Tulsa Riot Commission that did the first serious investigation into what happened in 1921.

The list of successful people who started at *Eagle* is long and distinguished.

Through the years, eight of my grandfather's children, grandchildren, and great-grandchildren would work at *The Eagle* in various roles from newspaper carriers, to staff writers, columnists, photographers, press operators, administrators, advertisers, circulators, and executives. My grandmother, Jeanne B. Goodwin, wore many hats at the newspaper, most notably writing a popular weekly column "Scoopin' the Scoop!" under the pen name, Ann Brown, for more than four decades.

In 2015, the Oklahoma Journalism Hall of Fame inducted my father and uncle, James Osby Goodwin, Sr., and Edward Lawrence Goodwin, Jr., respectively. Both served as editor and publisher after starting their careers as paper carriers. In 1986, my father told researcher Dr. Karen Brown Dunlap that *The Eagle's* vital role and relevance remains at our core today. "The paper will survive because of the purpose it serves. When I came to this position [as publisher] five years ago, I tried to find the purpose of the paper. The black press is still an alternative. It still talks about issues that are not addressed by metropolitan media. Its mission is as relevant today as in the days of *Freedom's Journal*."

In 2020, Robert Kerr "Bob" Goodwin was awarded the Hall of Fame's Lifetime Achievement Award. At 23, he left seminary early to assume leadership of the publishing company in 1972. Under his direction, *The Eagle* expanded to include editions in Muskogee, Okmulgee, Lawton,

James O. Goodwin, *The Oklahoma Eagle* publisher, continues a family newspaper legacy. Pictures in the background are of his brother Edward L. "Ed" Goodwin, Jr., his mother Jeanne B., and his father, E.L. Goodwin.

and in Wichita, Kansas; a Monday Morning *Eagle* edition; a weekly *Employment Central* edition; publishing opportunities; and operating an independent printing company, Pronto Print.

Bob is an entrepreneur, a college administrator, a former White House official with President George H.W. Bush, and an executive in the nonprofit arena. He served as president and CEO of the Points of Light Foundation, now Points of Light, an organization responsible for assisting and encouraging citizens to engage in volunteer service.

Despite a decline in newspaper readership and closures, *The Eagle* is the eleventh-oldest black-owned newspaper in the United States of 166 remaining publications affiliated with the National Newspaper Publishers Association.

In 2021, *The Eagle* will celebrate 100 years of continuous, uninterrupted weekly publication as we prepare to continue to produce a print product and expand our digital footprint.

BOB DOTSON
my (four) million miles
By Bob Dotson, 2019 Inductee

I've been in more motel rooms than the Gideon Bible, crisscrossing this country, practically nonstop, for half a century, searching for people who are practically invisible, the ones who change our lives, but don't take time to tweet and tell us about it.

America not only survives, but thrives because of all those names we don't know, seemingly ordinary people who do extraordinary things. They don't run for president or go on talk shows, but they are the heartbeat of this country.

As a young reporter, I began to wonder why we didn't dig deeper for stories about people who were not well-known. Assignment editors only sent me to interview ordinary Americans after something had shattered their lives.

If we only pay attention when tragedy strikes, sadness begins to seem normal. It is not.

Nothing is more American than optimism that overcomes hardship. Nothing is more valuable than tracking the course these ordinary people took to a better life. Give them the same investigative scrutiny as you would the mayor or city council. You'll be surprised what you uncover.

The American Dream reveals itself, not in what people say, but in what they do. Reporting often takes me out beyond the limits of my settled life. I've been to places so cold, spit bounces, chasing sled dogs 1,100 miles across Alaska. I've covered politics and breaking news. Shot documentaries. Ducked bullets reporting wars. I'm thankful every day that I've had time to pack a bag and go.

NBC News gave me a front row seat to history, but I prefer places the history books often overlook, towns small enough to consider Dairy Queen gourmet dining.

That's where you find the unexpected: Amish kids wearing inline skates and Civil War buffs fighting battles until the concession stands close.

The lights and shadows left a rich load of impressions.

Mention Mule Shoe, Texas, and a sign pops to mind: "Taxidermist and Veterinarian—either way you get your dog back."

Same with Blue Eye, Arkansas. Idling at a stoplight one afternoon, I read this in the window of a photographer's studio: "If you have beauty, I'll take it. If you have none, I'll fake it."

And then back when the earth was cooling, I made a film about Oklahoma Cheyenne Indians that featured Katie Osage, one of the oldest members of the tribe at the time.

After interviewing her, I plopped my earphones on her head so she could listen to herself.

Native American artist Louis Still Smoking saw my picture on Facebook nearly a half-century later. He was inspired to paint a portrait.

I saw it as I wandered through the Buffalo Bill Center in Cody, Wyoming.

What a surprise. A distant memory captured on canvas for future generations to see.

My knowledge of America is not bound in books.

Here's what I've learned traveling more than four million miles: The shortest distance between two people is a good story. Once you know someone's story, you see what you have in common. You begin to understand each other. That's important for a functioning democracy.

Most of what you hear on the news these days outlines our frustrations—the widening gap between the haves and the have-nots, middle class jobs fading away, hate-filled politics that prefers gridlock to compromise. What we know about America mostly comes from journalists who travel in herds, trailing politicians or camped out at big stories, pouncing on problems to repeat over and over. They offer up celebrity experts for solutions, the people who spend their busy days spouting opinions to cameras, while others in the shadows quietly make America work.

I spent my entire career peeking behind the media mirror that reflects celebrity and power, seeking those seemingly ordinary people who had already solved some problems we all face. Many had no riches but their thoughts. Their eyes grew rusty when they realized that poverty is inherited, just like wealth and then shined with renewed determination when someone with a barefoot voice helped them do better than they thought they could.

That's why America continues to build, discover, create, achieve, survive, and grow.

Wisdom doesn't always wear a suit.

Bob Dotson interviewing Oklahoma Cheyenne Katie Osage for the WKY-TV News Special titled *Until it's not here no more*. Katie Osage was hard of hearing. Dotson would ask his question an inch from her ear and then step out of the picture for her to answer. Bob Dotson, 1975.

Bob Dotson in Tennessee, videotaping *American Story* for NBC News. Pictured left to right: Rob Kane, sound; Allan Stecker, camera; Bob Dotson, News Correspondent; and Bert Medley, *Today Show* Producer. Photo courtesy of NBC, 1979.

Bob Dotson editing "Until it's not here no more" after winning Oklahoma's first National Emmy in 1974 for *Through the Looking Glass Darkly*, a 90-minute documentary on the history of African Americans in Oklahoma. Photo by Jim Hulsey, WKY-TV, 1974.

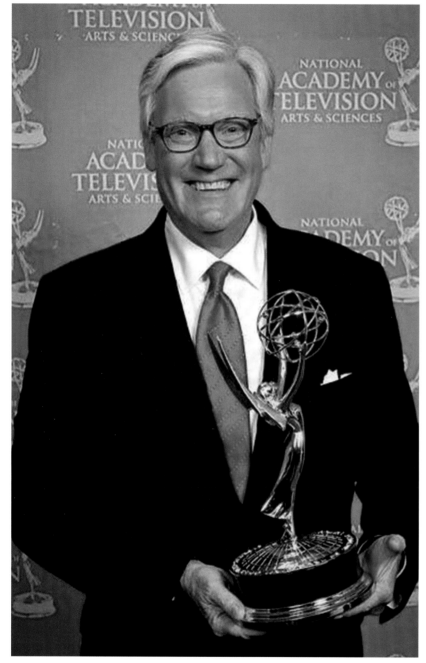

Bob Dotson holding his eighth National Emmy in 2010. He was nominated 11 times for his *American Story* series on the NBC *Today Show*. Photo courtesy of the National Academy of Television Arts and Science.

Bob Dotson checking his notebook before filing a story from western Oklahoma for WKY Radio. Photo by Jim Hulsey, WKY-TV, 1972.

ANTHONY SHADID

the friendly, genuine, two-time Pulitzer Prize-winning journalist

By Joe Hight, 2013 Inductee

My mind wandered when Anthony Shadid's name was read for induction into the Oklahoma Journalism Hall of Fame in 2012. All I could think about is what he had said to me the year before.

"Joe, I think this will be my last stint in the Middle East. I want to be here for my children."

The induction into the Hall of Fame was well-deserved for a journalist considered among the greatest of all foreign correspondents. But it was sad, too, considering what he had said to me and coming only two months after he died at age 43 of an apparent asthma attack. He had been trying to cross the Syrian border after spending a week there reporting for *The New York Times*.

Shadid and I had connected during his trips back to his native Oklahoma City. He would return to talk about his experiences in reporting in the Middle East or to provide training to students or fellow journalists.

His wife, Nada Bakri, said in an interview with *Democracy Now* after his death that she was struck in how modest he was when she met him in 2006. By that time, he already had won one Pulitzer Prize in 2004 for his coverage of the U.S. invasion of Iraq and its aftermath. He would win another in 2010. The Pulitzer board noted that he was able "to capture, at his own peril, the voices and emotions of Iraqis." His coverage was "rich, beautifully written."

Bakri also talked about "how nice he was," how he always made time for people, how he always listened to them. It was his trademark as a reporter and as an individual. "The Anthony I knew was a hard-working journalist who never turned anyone down."

He always seemed willing to stay that way when he returned to Oklahoma, even as his fame grew. But I also understood his deeper side, one involving his own heritage. After one of the times he spoke at *The Oklahoman*, I drove him back to his childhood home. We started talking about his last name and how it was pronounced. In Oklahoma, he said, it was "Sha-DID." But outside of Oklahoma, it was "Sha-DEED."

He said in an interview on a *Thousand and One Journeys: The Arab American Experience* that he felt Lebanese Americans had to assimilate into the community, into the state of Oklahoma. That they were "not wanting to be too different." That was the reasoning he gave me for the pronunciation of his last name here. At the same time, as he stated in the interview, he was "proud of being Lebanese … Proud of being Arab American."

He seemed fearless as a journalist, too. He kept returning on assignment to the Middle East despite being shot in the shoulder as he walked on a street in the West Bank in 2002, despite fearing for his life after being kidnapped and tortured by the pro-government militia in Libya for more than a week in 2011, despite being harassed during riots in Egypt that same year.

He said in the *Thousand and One Journeys* interview that it was "painful as a journalist" to cover the human tragedy in the Middle East. He admitted, "I don't like covering conflict."

But he did it because he found friendly people whenever he was on assignment there. He found "how gentle" the Middle East can be.

That was a trait that I believe he found in most places he visited. A trait that made him among the friendliest and most genuine journalists I had ever met.

After the induction ceremony in 2012, I searched for a book that Anthony had signed for me. It was the paperback of the *Night Draws Near,* which won the 2005 *Los Angeles Times* Book Prize.

He wrote on October 4, 2010: "To Joe: A great friend in Oklahoma! Wishing best regards, Anthony Shadid."

I suspect that's what he was to everyone he knew, wherever he traveled: A great friend. That's how I'll remember him.

JOE HIGHT

the snow/ice storm and the will to attend an induction ceremony

By Joe Hight, 2013 Inductee

Snow and ice were predicted in Colorado on April 17, 2013. I told my wife, Nan, that we had to make it to my Oklahoma Journalism Hall of Fame induction by the next morning.

Even with a four-wheel-drive Buick Enclave, a white-out had stopped us only three weeks before, just outside Pueblo.

This time, we avoided the storm the best we could. We drove winding two-lane roads. But the inevitable occurred: It snowed. Ice fell. We stopped for gasoline at a convenience store.

After I paid, a man I didn't know asked me, "Is that your red SUV?"

"Yes," I replied.

"Well, it's completely covered in ice."

The Enclave was covered in ice. We pressed on. Snow and ice wouldn't stop us from attending the induction luncheon.

I doubt snow and ice would stop any journalist from being inducted into the Hall of Fame.

OLIVER MURRAY

a Hall of Fame photojournalist—and mentor

By John Greiner, 1993 Inductee

Oliver Murray, the first African-American photojournalist in Oklahoma City, was much more than a television news photographer.

Murray, who worked for Oklahoma City's WKY, now known as KFOR-TV, was a political reporter and tutor for young television reporters whom he accompanied to the Oklahoma State Capitol, often on their first assignments there.

The Capitol can be imposing to young reporters making their first news conference involving politics and armed only with news clippings on what would be the subject.

If Murray noticed the young reporter from his station struggling, he would ask the question himself or tell the reporter what to ask.

Murray was up to date on all politics, local and national.

The smarter reporters assigned with him learned early to listen to his suggestions.

During his 38-year career, Murray held many positions, including chief news photographer and operations manager.

More than 50 years ago when we met, he was not only the photographer. He also filed stories to WKY Radio.

He, Bob Dotson, and George Wesley teamed to produce a documentary on black history that won three Emmys. Titled *Through the Looking Glass Darkly,* it ran in a series on WKY Television.

Murray also was instrumental in starting the local chapter of the Association of Black Journalists.

Oliver Murray was inducted into the Oklahoma Journalism Hall of Fame in 2013.

THE INVESTIGATIVE REPORTERS

the Hall of Famers who fearlessly worked to expose wrongdoing

By Mary Hargrove, 2018 Inductee

I was 24 years old when the *Tulsa Tribune* hired me in the fall of 1974. I insisted I wanted to be an investigative reporter. President Richard Nixon had resigned six months earlier, following two years of dogged reporting by Bob Woodward and Carl Bernstein at *The Washington Post.*

"We will never have enough money or manpower for a full-time investigator," I was told as they assigned me to the education beat.

Ten years later, I was projects editor with a two-reporter team at the *Tulsa Tribune* and had been elected to the board of Investigative Reporters & Editors.

I was not the first investigative reporter in Oklahoma and definitely not the last.

Over the past 50 years, Oklahoma Journalism Hall of Fame members such as Griff Palmer, Jerry Bohnen, Robby Trammell, Terri Watkins, Nolan Clay, Randy Ellis, and Ziva Branstetter fearlessly broke ground in the rapidly evolving world of investigations.

Their nationally recognized projects exposed kickbacks involving more than 240 county commissioners and their material suppliers; mishandling of millions of dollars by televangelist Oral Roberts; the failure of Penn Square Bank in Oklahoma City which led to the country's largest bank bailout at that time; and the use of questionable drugs in the botched execution of Clayton Lockett.

Sometimes, the work was painfully personal.

Most of these reporters covered the April 19, 1995, bombing of the Alfred P. Murrah Federal Building in Oklahoma City, where the bodies of 168 people, including 19 children, were extracted from the rubble.

"It breaks your heart and brands your soul," wrote columnist Berry Tramel, also a Hall of Fame member.

Some spent years tracking the activities of the two men responsible for the nation's worst domestic terrorist attack before September 11, 2001.

These reporters collectively have won hundreds of contests, earning two Pulitzer Prizes, two Peabody Awards, and two Investigative Reporters & Editors awards. They can also claim the grand-prize Robert F. Kennedy Award, the Heywood Broun, and an Edward R. Murrow Award.

Reporters following the money trail helped end the careers of numerous politicians, including longtime Department of Human Services Director Lloyd Rader, Sr. and State Treasurer Claudette Henry. *The Oklahoman* stunned the state when it revealed the secret indictment of Governor David Walters for conspiring to hide campaign contributions.

Robby Trammell uncovered one of the most brazen misuse of funds when he wrote about the gross overstaffing of a state home for juveniles, where 172 employees were caring for 13 children.

Investigative reporting was primitive when most of us tackled our first projects.

In the 1970s and 1980s we worked without cell phones, laptops, fax machines, or the Internet. Collecting data involved dozens of phone calls to find studies and relevant records which might arrive weeks later in the mail.

Following tips, reporters crisscrossed the state tracking con men and their victims. We combed through dusty file drawers in turn-of-the-century courthouses or squinted at blurry microfilm with no idea what we might find. Broadcast equipment was bulky and cumbersome.

The few women working in "hard news" faced additional challenges.

During a break in an Oklahoma City civil damages trial in 1979, I found four male reporters interviewing the plaintiff's attorney over lunch. I asked if I could join them. The attorney scooted his hotel room key across the table. "You and I can have a special interview later," he said, winking.

His key was "accidentally" dropped and kicked across the restaurant floor as I left.

New technology upped the quality and impact of investigations in the 1990s. Griff Palmer became *The Oklahoman's* first database editor in 1994.

As the Internet expanded in the new millennium, our in-depth stories spread across the country.

Technology also doomed a large segment of the media.

A staggering 2,100 newspapers closed between 2004 and 2019. Ironically, investigative reporting, once deemed a luxury, became an industry-saving necessity.

Online media offered a critical outlet.

Since 2010, Oklahoma has witnessed the advent of digital journalism startups including Oklahoma Watch, The Frontier, This Land, and NonDoc.

These sites—while different in many ways—provided important alternative outlets for enterprise and investigative stories.

Ziva Branstetter left the *Tulsa World* and helped create The Frontier in April 2015. The online investigative newspaper proliferated, going from zero to 1.5 million individual hits per month during her first two years as editor.

Today, the once fiercely competitive newspapers and broadcasters collaborate, sharing each other's investigations in print and online, locally and nationally.

What can't be measured, what hasn't changed, is the heart and soul of investigative reporting: finding justice for the vulnerable.

The images linger.

An elderly woman in a mental health facility raising her floor-length skirt to reveal deep purple bruises inflicted by the staff.

A 12-year-old boy walking in front of a semi-truck on the interstate rather than return home where his mother's boyfriend sexually abused him.

A firefighter cradling a dying baby girl in his arms after the Oklahoma City bombing.

My friends often asked why I worked so hard. Why I exposed myself to threats, the stress, the intimate nightmares of strangers that pierce your psyche in the middle of the night? Why didn't I just walk away?

The truth is simple. People were being cheated, abused, or killed. Once you know, how can you walk away?

You can't. And we didn't.

Terri Watkins was inducted in 2005, Jerry Bohnen in 2006, Robby Trammell in 2015, Nolan Clay and Randy Ellis in 2016, and Ziva Branstetter and Griff Palmer in 2019. Berry Tramel joined the Hall of Fame in 2018.

Some of the media representatives who witnessed Charles Troy Coleman's execution were, from left, Ron Jenkins, Dan Rutherford, Randy Mosier, Ziva Branstetter, Robby Trammell, Paul Sund, Jacqueline Scott, and Kelly Ogle. Photo by Jim Argo. September 10, 1990. Courtesy of the Oklahoma Historical Society.

Mary Hargrove running investigations at the *Tulsa Tribune* in 1988. In 1986 and 1987, she covered Oral Roberts and his finances, exposing his misuse of funds that nearly collapsed the university.

Oklahoma's lawmakers and government officials were under the watchful eyes of the press in this undated photo.

Chris Casteel, *The Oklahoman*, interviews then Vice President George H.W. Bush at the National Cowboy Hall of Fame in Oklahoma City during a campaign stop. February 1988.

Chris Casteel (right) questioned then Vice President Al Gore about meeting with moderate Democrats on reforming government. This interview was in the Rayburn House Office Building on Capitol Hill in Washington, D.C. September 1993.

Chris Casteel (right) interviews then Oklahoma Governor David Walters in East Lansing, Michigan after a presidential debate. Walters was there to provide "spin" for Bill Clinton. October 1992.

"Ed Montgomery taps out new newsroom's first story for fellow staffer Mike McCarville to photograph." July 13, 1963. Courtesy of the Oklahoma Historical Society.

Lilian Newby, Theta Sigma Phi president and reporter for the *Tulsa Tribune*, checks her notes for a story on the Legislature. Photo by Joe Miller. March 4, 1971. Courtesy of the Oklahoma Historical Society.

Otis Sullivant. Photo by Dick Cobb. August 4, 1961.

'I GUESS I'VE GOT EGG ON MY FACE'

the tape confirms it

By John Greiner, 1993 Inductee

In Governor David Hall's second year in office, he launched an ambitious road program called "Freeway 77" aimed at building and repairing highways and bridges in all 77 counties.

The media pressed Hall on which roads and how much money would be spent in each county.

Hall told Chester Brooks, the state highway director, to produce the information. But Brooks told me when I was at *The Oklahoman* that the Highway Department was not ready.

The media continued to push—as did the governor—and the highway program was delivered later in the week to the press room.

But there were flaws pointed out by *The Oklahoman's* Paul English, *The Oklahoman's* Jim Standard, and the *Tulsa World's* Chuck Ervin.

English was the only reporter who used a tape recorder in those days. With his tape running, he told Brooks what was wrong.

"I guess I've got egg on my face," Brooks said.

That phrase inflamed Hall and in less than a week, Hall had Brooks before a news conference to denounce what he had said.

Hall asked Brooks if he ever said, "I have egg on my face." Brooks emphatically said, "No sir!"

English left the news conference and ran up the stairs to the press room.

He returned, sat in his usual chair and asked Hall to listen to the tape.

With the governor listening, English rolled the tape and it clearly said, " … I've got egg on my face."

The governor then responded to his audience of reporters: "See, he didn't say it!"

RALPH SCHAEFER
'The Longest Wait' for Hall of Fame membership
By Ralph Schaefer, 2017 Inductee

The Longest Day is a war movie starring John Wayne.

The Longest Yard is a prison/sports movie starring Burt Reynolds.

"The Longest Wait" isn't a movie—and never will be.

It's a "title" unknowingly held by *me*, a Tulsa journalist, because of my 16-year wait to be inducted into the Oklahoma Journalism Hall of Fame.

"What!" was my surprised reaction when told I was the subject of "The Longest Wait."

I had first been nominated in 2001 and would be nominated a second time before being inducted into the "Land of Media Giants" on April 27, 2017.

Joe Hight, Oklahoma Journalism Hall of Fame Director and 2013 inductee, was delighted to say I was the subject for "The Longest Wait" as planning for this book began.

I had no idea I would be the subject and writing about myself.

But I am honored to be a member of this organization.

Graduating from Central State College in December 1969—the name changed to Central State University on January 1, 1970—my newspaper career in community journalism began with the *El Reno Daily Tribune* in 1969.

Publisher Jack Dyer, on my first day on the job, waved his hand over El Reno and said, "This is your beat, cover it."

In 1973, Bill Retherford drove me around Tulsa, introduced me to his three newspaper offices and, in effect, said, "These are your beats."

I left Tulsa briefly and worked at *The Journal Record* in 1980, learning to write about business and the legal community.

I returned to Tulsa and Retherford Publications in 1981 to become part of a growing newspaper group, a role that continued until the publisher's death in 2005.

Repeat that "cover it" scenario when Community Publishers Inc. owners opened the *Tulsa Business Journal and Legal News* office at Fifth and Boston in downtown Tulsa.

I was tasked with covering Tulsa's legal community.

I retired in 2018 when the *Tulsa Daily Legal News* ceased publication after 109 years.

Looking back, I worked nearly 49 years in a profession to give a voice to people and serve their communities.

I am proud to be a journalist and am proud to be an Oklahoma Journalism Hall of Fame member.

That long wait, even if I didn't know it at first, was worth it.

MEMBERS INDUCTED FROM 2010 TO 2019

— 2010

Gean B. Atkinson (1944-), author of three books, advertising agency owner, served in the Oklahoma Legislature, decorated Vietnam veteran of the U.S. Marine Corps, director of the Joint Information Bureau of the United Arab Emirates during Operation Desert Shield/ Storm as a Navy captain, corporate communications director for Express Personnel Services, journalism instructor at the University of Central Oklahoma.

Mike Boettcher (1954-), worked with WBBZ, KEBC, KTOK, and KWTV, CNN war correspondent in the Mideast, chief correspondent for CNN's terrorism investigation unit, reporter for NBC, ABC, BBC, and *The Oklahoman*, recipient of a Peabody Award, several National Emmy awards, and a National Headliner Award.

Ray Dyer (1957-), co-publisher of the *El Reno Tribune* and *Mustang News*, reporter at the *Southwest Times Record* in Fort Smith, Arkansas, covered sports at the *McAlester Capital-Democrat*, editor of the *Sooner Catholic*, served on several Oklahoma Press Association committees, among other boards.

Sean Dyer (1960-), co-publisher of the *El Reno Tribune* and *Mustang News*, third-generation Oklahoma Press Association president (2001), worked with the *Piedmont Gazette* and *Okarche Chieftain*, president of the Oklahoma Newspaper Foundation, chairman of the OPA-MEBT insurance trust, president of the El Reno Rotary Club.

Susan Boling Ellerbach (1955-), executive editor, managing editor, business writer, business editor, state editor, and Sunday editor for the *Tulsa World*, editor at the *Tahlequah Daily Press*, managing editor of the *Tahlequah American*, president of Associated Press/Oklahoma Newspaper Executives, served on the Blue Cross/Blue Shield Caring Program for Children and the Child Abuse Network boards.

Melba Lovelace (1930-), secretary for the Oklahoma Publishing Company, wrote the daily column "Melba's Swap Shop" for *The Daily Oklahoman*, hosted TV shows, a regular radio show, and taught cooking classes at UCO, wrote 16 books on recipes, crafting, quilting, and household hints.

John A. "Andy" Rieger (1957-), managing editor for the *Norman Transcript*, worked with the *Oklahoma Daily* and the *Oklahoma City Times*, co-founder of a weekly newspaper in Noble, adviser to the *Oklahoma Daily*, chairman of the advisory committee of the Ethics and Excellence in Journalism Foundation.

Bill Sherman (1945-), copy editor, assistant city editor, night editor, and religion writer for the *Tulsa World*, worked with the *Albuquerque Journal* and the *Burlington Standard Press*, named second in the nation in the Religion Newswriters Association, honored with the Russell Bennett Faith and Courage Award from the Tulsa Interfaith Alliance.

Jack Stone (1937-), executive editor for the *Anadarko Daily News,* covered cops for the *Tulsa Tribune,* wrote "The Cornerstone," a column that appeared in *The Daily News* for 30 years, recipient of the Oklahoma Press Association's Beachy Musselman Award.

— 2011

Gloria G. Brown (1942-), women's editor, managing editor, and editor for the *Perry Daily Journal,* named Perry Citizen of the Year, Perry Business Woman of the Year, Beta Sigma Phi Woman of the Year and parade marshal at the annual Cherokee Strip parade, secretary treasurer for the Assembly of God church.

Jeff Dixon (1945-), worked with *The Lawton Constitution* and *Morning Press,* recipient of numerous awards from the Oklahoma Press Association and the Associated Press, named Artist of the Year by the Lawton Arts and Humanities Council (2006), member of the World War II Aerial Demonstration Team of Frederick, photography and photojournalism professor.

Arnold Hamilton (1958-), editor of *The Oklahoma Observer,* Oklahoma bureau chief for the *Dallas Morning News,* two-time winner of the Dallas Press Club Katie Award, recipient of the Fran Morris Civil Liberties in Media Award, worked with the *San Jose Mercury News, Dallas Times Herald, Tulsa Tribune,* and *Oklahoma Journal.*

Joan Henderson (1956-), general manager and publisher of the award-winning *Oklahoma Today* Magazine, conference and webinar speaker, board member of several magazine associations, published photographer, worked in advertising, videodisc production, and multi-image slide production; media specialist at Vo-Tech in Stillwater.

Michael R. Jones (1949-), served the *Tulsa World* in many capacities, including oil writer, copy editor, assistant city editor, city editor, layout editor, editorial writer, associate editor, and columnist, honorary chief executive officer of his son's reggae-funk-rock band, Sam and the Stylees.

David Page (1949-), news editor, managing editor, and special projects editor for *The Journal Record,* helped publish a firsthand account of the 1995 Oklahoma City bombing, Associated Press/Oklahoma Newspaper Executives president, and recipient of its Carl Rogan Sweepstakes Award, reporter for the *Bristol Herald Courier, Bristol Virginia Tennessean,* and *West Side Story.*

Jim Standard (1940-2010), worked with the *Oklahoma City Times* and *The Oklahoman* in many capacities, including senior reporter, state capitol bureau chief, city editor, and executive editor, covered the assassination of President John F. Kennedy and named Oklahoma "Newsman of the Year" for his coverage, Nieman Fellow at Harvard.

Keith Swezey (1952-2019), worked with WKY and KOMA Radio, built the award-winning student broadcast program at the University of Central Oklahoma, where he also served as director of Academic Broadcasting Services, chairman of the Communication Department and adviser to the Old Bridge Education Association, recipient of Radio Television Digital News Association's Edward R. Murrow Award for best documentary.

Larry R. Wade (1939-2011), publisher of the *Elk City Daily News*, editor of the *Oklahoma Daily*, recipient of the University of Oklahoma Benefactor Award, chairman of the University of Oklahoma Board of Regents, Oklahoma Press Association president (1983), recipient of the Milt Phillips Award, founder of the Elk City Foundation, Western Oklahoma Hall of Fame inductee.

— 2012

Jim Ellis (1953-), sports editor of the *Miami News-Record* for more than 40 years, covered sports for the *Sequoyah County Times*, Oklahoma Eight-Man High School Football Hall of Fame inductee, Oklahoma Press Association Quarter Century Club member, recipient of a Mayoral Proclamation Award (2017).

Christy Gaylord Everest (1951-), third-generation leader of the Oklahoma Publishing Company, chairman of the University of Oklahoma Board of Regents, chairman of Casady School, Oklahoma Hall of Fame inductee, recipient of the Governor's Arts Award and the Casady School Distinguished Graduate Award, chairman of the University of Oklahoma Cancer Center Leadership Council.

Gerald C. Green (1939-), worked with the *Austin American-Statesman, Clinton Daily News,* and *Dallas Morning News,* served in the U.S. Air Force as base and wing information officer, news officer for the American Forces Korea Network and as Minuteman missile crew commander; editor of *The Ord Quiz.*

Neal Kennedy (1949-), worked with KCSC-FM, WKY, KRMC, KVOO, KRMG News, and the *Oklahoma Journal,* recipient of the Edward R. Murrow Award, president of the Associated Press and United Press International broadcasting associations, president of Oklahoma Sigma Delta Chi, broadcasting professor, announcer at the Hallett Motor Racing Circuit.

William C. "Bill" Morgan (1930-2012), worked with *The Daily O'Collegian, Bartlesville Record,* and *Henryetta Daily Free-Lance,* regional editor for the *Stars and Stripes* in the U.S. Army Press Corps, owner of the *Hughes County Times,* published *The Calvin Chronicle, Oklahoma Peanut,* and *The Weleetkan.*

Anthony Shadid (1968-2012), foreign correspondent for *The New York Times,* two-time Pulitzer Prize winner, Islamic affairs correspondent for *The Washington Post,* Middle East correspondent for the Associated Press, recipient of the Ridenhour Book Prize, 2011 recipient of an honorary Doctorate of Humane Letters from the American University of Beirut.

Stan Stamper (1953-), publisher of the family-owned *Hugo Daily News*, publisher of the *Choctaw County Times*, author of two aviation novels, namesake of the Stan Stamper Municipal Airport, named Oklahoma Aviator of the Year in (1997), chairman of the Oklahoma Aeronautics Commission, named Hugo Citizen of the Year (1994).

James D. Watts, Jr. (1961-), worked with the *Tulsa World*, covering the arts and winning multiple awards, worked with the *Broken Arrow Ledger, Lost Treasure Magazine, Continental Heritage Press,* and *Tulsa Tribune*, recipient of the Harwelden Award for contributions to the arts (2006).

Faith L. Wylie (1953-), co-publisher of the *Oologah Lake Leader*, co-winner of the Beachy Musselman Award, production artist at Sun Publications, graphic designer for BR Johnson Studio, art director at Old American Insurance Company, president of the Oologah Historical Society, named Chamber Citizen of the Year (1985).

John M. Wylie II (1953-), co-publisher of the *Oologah Lake Leader*, correspondent for the *Des Moines Register* and United Press International, news director of KDIC-FM, energy and environment writer for the *Kansas City Star*, which won a Pulitzer for coverage of the Hyatt disaster, co-winner of the Beachy Musselman Award, named Oologah Citizen of the Year (1991).

— 2013

James Coburn (1955-), investigative reporter and photographer for *The Edmond Sun*, annual writer for the Edmond HOPE Center project, recipient of two sweepstakes awards from the Associated Press, two-time winner of the American Cancer Society's High Plains Media Award, winner of the Edmond Historical Society Historic Preservation Award, and poetry book author.

Joe Hancock (1929-2014), publisher of the *Hobart Democrat-Chief*, worked for papers in Anadarko, Mangum, Frederick, and Duncan, operator at *The Norman Transcript* and *Oklahoma Daily*, named Hobart Citizen of the Year (1998), president of the Hobart Housing Board, president of the Oklahoma Press Association (1991), recipient of the Milt Phillips Award (2006).

Joe Hight (1958-), former managing editor/director of *The Oklahoman*, co-founder of the Dart Center for Journalism and Trauma, chairman of the Mid-America Press Institute, board member of Associated Press Media Editors, "Oklahoma Joe" columnist for *The Journal Record*, University of Central Oklahoma endowed journalism ethics chair, director of the Oklahoma Journalism Hall of Fame, Oklahoma Watch board chairman, Freedom of Information Oklahoma president, recipient of at least 20 national awards, including being editor of *The Gazette* in Colorado Springs, Colorado when it won the Pulitzer Prize in 2014, author and bookstore owner.

John Klein (1953-), senior sports columnist for the *Tulsa World*, covering NASCAR, boxing and golfing; sportswriter for the *Perry Daily Journal*, sports editor for the *Daily Ardmoreite*, covered the Southwest Conference for the *Houston Post*, named Oklahoma Sportswriter of the Year (2000).

Jerry Laizure (1953-2012), senior photographer at the *Norman Transcript*, worked for the *Bartlesville Examiner-Enterprise*, the *Oklahoma Daily*, and the *Oil and Gas Journal*, co-founder of the *Cleveland County Record*, winner of multiple photography awards from the Associated Press, the Society of Professional Journalists, and the Oklahoma Press Association.

Mike McCarville (1940-2017), started *The McCarville Report*, publisher of the *Del City News*, worked at the *Oklahoma Journal, Tulsa Tribune, Norman Transcript, Oklahoma Courier,* and *The Daily Oklahoman* and *Oklahoma City Times*, assistant news director of KWTV, investigative reporter, talk show host and program director for KTOK Radio, director of the National Association of Business Political Action Committees.

Mary Mélon (1961-), president and publisher of *The Journal Record*, senior management corporate team member of the Dolan Company, recipient of the Association for Women in Communications Byliner Award, recipient of the YWCA's Embrace Award, inducted into the Oklahoma City University Meinders School of Business Hall of Honor.

Tom Muchmore (1950-), third-generation publisher of *The Ponca City News* and *The Tonkawa News*, owner and manager of WBBZ Radio, president of poncacity.net, chairman of the Ponca City Area Chamber of Commerce, Lew Wentz Foundation trustee, recipient of Ponca City's Outstanding Citizen Award, president of the Oklahoma Press Association (1997), recipient of the Milt Phillips Award.

Oliver C. Murray (1941-), first African-American photojournalist in Oklahoma City, chief news photographer and production/operations manager at WKY-TV, directed the station's and Oklahoma's first "live truck," co-producer of an Emmy-winning documentary, helped start the local chapter of the Association of Black Journalists.

— 2014

Ed Blochowiak (1950-2016), photojournalist at the *Shawnee News-Star* for more than 40 years, served in Vietnam in the U.S. Air Force, winner of more than 90 photography awards from The Associated Press, Oklahoma Press Association, and other organizations; awarded Photo of the Year once by The Associated Press and twice by the Oklahoma Press Association.

Thomas H. "Tom" Boone (1936-), sportswriter for the *Bixby Bulletin* for almost 40 years, served in the U.S. Marine Corps and played baseball for the Marines, created the Bulletin's "Player of the Year" Award, Bixby Athletic Hall of Fame inductee, Oklahoma Press Association Quarter Century Club member, owner of a sports reporting company.

Jay Cronley (1943-2017), columnist for the *Tulsa World*, sports writer for *The Daily Oklahoman*, sportswriter and columnist for the *Tulsa Tribune*, horse racing columnist for ESPN, author of eight novels, winner of a national non-fiction writing award from *Playboy* Magazine, inducted into the Oklahoma Writers Hall of Fame.

Carolyn Estes (1943-), marketing director at the *Oologah Lake Leader*, where she also developed the Newspapers in Education program, recipient of the President's Award from the Oklahoma Press Association, Oklahoma Newspaper Foundation board member, president of the Chamber of Commerce, recipient of many awards, including the town's Community Spirit Award, Spirit of Will Rogers Award, and the Oklahoma Educators Association Marshall Gregory Award.

Larry Ferguson (1937-), co-publisher of the *Cleveland American* and the *Hominy Progress*, publisher of the *Pawnee Chief*, elected to the Oklahoma House of Representatives, serving as Minority Leader from 1991-1998, Oklahoma Press Association Half Century Club member, president of the Oklahoma State School Board Association.

Kelly Dyer Fry (1959-), editor and publisher of *The Oklahoman*, vice president of news for OPUBCO Communications Group, director of multimedia at *The Oklahoman*, leading the team that launched NewsOK in 2001, worked with her family newspaper, the *El Reno Tribune*, worked with *The Daily O'Collegian*, served on multiple education boards.

William A. Hamilton (1935-), worked with the *Anadarko Daily News*, Master Parachutist, earning the Silver Star, Distinguished Flying Cross, 20 Air Medals, four Bronze Stars, and the Purple Heart, editor-in-chief of the *Lincoln Capital Times*, featured commentator for *USA Today*, co-author of four spy novels, Oklahoma Army ROTC Wall of Fame, Oklahoma Military Hall of Fame, and Colorado Aviation Hall of Fame inductee.

Tim Schnoebelen (1944-), third-generation journalist, publisher of the family-owned *Mooreland Leader*, wrote for the student newspaper at Northwestern State College (now Northwestern Oklahoma State University), worked with the *Oklahoma Daily*, served on numerous Oklahoma Press Association committees, recipient of the Milt Phillips Award and the University of Oklahoma Regents' Award.

Jan Stratton (1940-), anchor, news director, and public affairs director for KSWO-TV in Lawton, executive producer, co-producer, writer, and anchor for 7 News, performed with the Lawton Community Theatre and Lawton Philharmonic Orchestra, recipient of an Orange County Transporation Association acting award, Oklahoma Association of Broadcasters Hall of Fame inductee.

— 2015

Julie DelCour (1951-), associate editor for the *Tulsa World*, worked with newspapers in Springfield (Missouri), covered the Oklahoma City bombing investigation and trials, named Newsmaker of the Year from the Association for Women in Communications, named one of the 100 Women With Moxie by the Tulsa YWCA in 2014.

Edward L. "Ed" Goodwin, Jr. (1935-2014), editor and publisher of *The Oklahoma Eagle* in Tulsa, worked with other newspapers in Tulsa and Kansas City, Missouri, active in the civil rights movement in the 1950s and 1960s, worked to preserve the historic Greenwood District in Tulsa.

James O. Goodwin (1939-), publisher and editor of *The Oklahoma Eagle*, attorney at law, recipient of the Tulsa Press Club Print Icon Award, The University of Tulsa College of Law Hall of Fame inductee, namesake of the James O. Goodwin Health Center, co-counsel in the matter of reparation for victims of the 1921 Tulsa race massacre.

Ron Hagler (1940-), news film cameraman at KSWO-TV in Lawton, chief photographer for KOTV in Tulsa, co-owner of Hagler-Callaway Productions for 17 years, freelance technician for CBS, was part of an Emmy award winning team covering the Mexico City earthquake in 1985.

John A. Hruby (1964-2014), co-publisher of the *Marlow Review* and *Comanche County Chronicle*, third-generation Oklahoma journalist, publisher of the *Duncan Banner*, active in the Oklahoma Press Association, vice president of the Oklahoma Newspaper Foundation's board of trustees.

Joy "Tinker" Hruby (1966-2014), co-publisher of the *Marlow Review* and co-owner of the *Comanche County Chronicle*, taught second grade in Duncan, worked in real estate, banking, and as a private investigator, worked with her husband to produce a quality newspaper and was active in both Marlow and Duncan.

Rose Lane (1962-), managing editor, general manager, and deputy publisher of *FRIDAY*, assistant news director for KRMS/KYLC Radio in Osage Beach, Missouri, reporter for the *Reveille/Lake Sun Leader*, editor and sales executive for *Vacation News*, recipient of the Oklahoma Press Association Quarter Century Club award.

Patrick B. McGuigan (1954-), writer for *The O'Collegian*, editor and publisher of *The City Sentinel*, founder of CapitolBeatOK.com, writer for *Perspective* Magazine, editor of *The Initiative and Referendum Report* in Washington, directed *The Oklahoman* editorial page, state secretary-treasurer for the Society of Professional Journalists, author of three books.

Gary Reid (1936-), publisher of the *Kingfisher Times & Free Press*, worked with the *Pauls Valley Daily Democrat*, editor of the *Wewoka Daily News*, owner of the *Hollis News*, recipient of the Oklahoma Press Association Beachy Musselman Award and the Society of Professional Journalists First Amendment Award, named Kingfisher Citizen of the Year in 2002.

Jenifer Reynolds (1958-), co-host of the television show *Discover Oklahoma,* winner of the DuPont-Columbia Award, worked with KOSU-FM, WKY-AM, and KWTV-TV, recipient of the Lifetime Achievement Award from the American Women in Radio and Television in 2001.

Judy Gibbs Robinson (1956-), assistant director of Student Media and editorial adviser to the *Oklahoma Daily* at the University of Oklahoma, worked with the *Columbia Daily Tribune*, Missouri, worked with The Associated Press in several states, minority affairs reporter at *The Oklahoman*, named a College Media Association Honor Roll Adviser (2012).

Robby Trammell (1952-), news director for *The Oklahoman* and NewsOK.com, editor of the papers at Seminole High School and Seminole Junior College, reporter and managing editor of the *Seminole Producer*, leader of *The Oklahoman's* Tulsa bureau, award-winning investigative reporter.

— 2016

Louise Abercrombie (1935-), business editor of *The Ponca City News*, covering all facets of community news; columnist, photographer, first woman named Outstanding Citizen of Ponca City, named Oklahoma SBA Journalist of the Year, Oklahoma Press Association Beachy Musselman Award recipient.

Bob Barry, Jr. (1956-2015), sports director for KFOR-TV and KAUT-TV, hosted the talk radio show "Sports Morning" on Oklahoma City's WWLS-AM/FM, created the Channel 4 basketball team, "The Foul Shots," named Oklahoma Sportscaster of the Year six times by the National Sportscasters and Sportswriters Association.

Virginia Bradshaw (1929-), worked with the *Countywide & Sun, Chandler News-Publicist, Norman Transcript, Shawnee News-Star, Woodward Daily Press, Alva Review-Courier, Anadarko Daily News, Oklahoma Daily,* and *The Oklahoman*, author of two books, Oklahoma Press Association Quarter and Half Century clubs member.

Nolan Clay (1959-), investigative reporter for *The Oklahoman*, with more than 100 state, regional, and national awards for excellence, covered the Oklahoma City bombing and trials, consultant for the Oklahoma City National Memorial & Museum, worked with the *Sulphur Times-Democrat* and the *Tulsa Tribune*.

Randy Ellis (1955-), investigative reporter for *The Oklahoman*, helping to expose corruption in higher education, gubernatorial campaign financing, county government, school bond financing, the Oklahoma Legislature, and other offices, recipient of more than 110 awards, worked with the *Arkansas Gazette* and the *Southwest Times Record*.

Janet Pearson (1954-), worked with the *Tulsa World*, covering energy, poverty, transportation, medicine, economic development, and social services, named associate editor in 2007, played a major role leading the world's fight against cockfighting, earning the Genesis Award from the National Humane Society.

Bill Perry (1950-), worked with OETA, KTEN-TV, KOCO-TV, KTEN, KAUT, KDFW-TV, WAVE-TV, WBBH-TV, and WATE-TV, recipient of eight regional Emmy Awards and two Western Heritage Wrangler Awards, regional vice president of the Heartland Chapter Emmy Awards, inducted into the "Silver Circle" of the Heartland Emmy Chapter.

Kenneth O. Reid (1926-), co-owner of the *Pauls Valley Daily Democrat, Wewoka Daily Times,* and *Frederick Daily Leader,* owner of the *Weatherford Daily News, Vinita Daily Journal, Nowata Star, Perry Daily Journal, Kingfisher Times & Free-Press,* and the *Sand Springs Leader and Times,* served as district Rotary governor, Oklahoma Press Association president (1979).

Rita L. Sherrow (1950-), *TV World* editor and television editor with the *Tulsa World* for more than three decades, TV columnist for *Weekend* Magazine, feature writer for the *Tulsa World's* Scene section, volunteer at the Tulsa State Fair as assistant horse superintendent and at the SPCA as a dog socializer.

— 2017

James Beaty (1952-), managing editor at the *McAlester News-Capital,* winner of two Associated Press sweepstakes awards for investigating city hall corruption, award-winning columnist, artist-in-residence for the Oklahoma Arts and Humanities Council, editor of East Central University's literary magazine, recipient of the Paul Hughes Award, as well as other state awards.

Steve Booher (1947-2017), worked with the *Winfield Daily Courier, Cherokee Messenger & Republican, Fairview Republican, Duncan Banner, Clinton Daily News,* and *Custer County Leader,* president of the Oklahoma Press Association (2008) and recipient of the Beachy Musselman Award, recipient of a Lifetime Achievement Award from the Cherokee Chamber of Commerce.

John Durkee (1955-), news director for KRMG, communications director for the city of Tulsa, news director for The University of Tulsa's KWGS Radio station, regular guest on RSU-TV public affairs programs, named 2016 Media Icon by the Tulsa Press Club, worked with KTOK, KAKC, and KFSB, two-time winner of the Radio Television Digital News Association's Edward R. Murrow Award.

Lis Exon (1956-), worked with OETA-TV, KJRH, KXXO, and KELI Radio in Tulsa, WESH in Orlando, KUSA in Denver, and KTRK in Houston, reporter for CNN, NBC, and ABC, recipient of an Investigative Reporters and Editors Inc. award, the Colby Award, the Texas Governor's Award and many Society of Professional Journalists awards, including being honored twice for having the Best Reporter Portfolio.

Carla Hinton (1966-), religion editor at *The Oklahoman,* named 2009 Journalist of the Year by the Tulsa Association of Black Journalists, recipient of the Excellence in Religious Journalism Award by the Oklahoma Conference of Churches and the Friend of Faith Award from the Oklahoma Church of Jesus Christ of the Latter-Day Saints, Oklahoma African-American Hall of Fame inductee.

 **Randy Krehbiel** (1956-), worked with the *Oklahoma City Times* and the *Marion Chronicle-Tribune*, sports and news writer for the *Tulsa World*, covering everything from college football and boxing to higher education and politics; covered the Tulsa Race Riot Commission and the John Hope Franklin Commission, author.

 **Dr. Paul R. Lehman** (1941-), first African-American newsperson on Oklahoma City television at KWTV-9, co-creator and host of the "Soul Talk" show, English professor and dean of the graduate college at the University of Central Oklahoma, author of numerous books, listed in *Who's Who Among Black Americans* and in American Education.

 **Ralph Schaefer** (1939-), associate editor for *Southeast News, Tulsa County News,* and the *Owasso Reporter,* worked on all papers in the Retherford Publications group, senior editor for the combined *Tulsa Daily Business Journal* and the *Tulsa Daily Commerce and Legal News*, recipient of the Liberty Bell Award, Executive Committee member for the Oklahoma Journalism Hall of Fame.

 **Gene Triplett** (1949-), longest-serving city editor at *The Oklahoman* (1989-1999), worked with *The Oklahoma Journal*, president of The Associated Press News Executives board, listed in *Who's Who in America*, inducted into the Oklahoma Music Hall of Fame, contributing founder of the Oklahoma Film Critics Circle, author of novels, including *Wheel Man.*

— **2018**

 **Jon Denton** (1940-), fourth-generation member of a printing, publishing, and newspaper family, started the *Sunday Showcase Magazine*, Kellogg Grant recipient, assistant city editor of the *Oklahoma City Times*, managing editor of the metro *EASTnews* and *SOUTHnews*, managing editor of *The Guthrie Daily Leader.*

 **Mary Hargrove** (1950-), worked with the *Newark Advocate, Miami Herald, Arkansas Democrat-Gazette,* and *Tulsa Tribune*, where she covered the Penn Square Bank collapse in Oklahoma City, treasurer, vice president, president, and chair of Investigative Reporters and Editors, recipient of the Robert F. Kennedy grand prize.

 **Barbara Hoberock** (1966-), served at the *Tulsa Tribune* as Capitol Bureau chief, longest-serving Oklahoma statehouse reporter and as dean of the Capitol Press Corps, worked with the *Claremore Daily Progress*, Oklahoma State University's *O'Collegian,* and the *Tulsa World*, where she covered the Oklahoma City bombing and trials.

 **Douglas Hoke** (1956-), Oklahoma Interscholastic Press Association Photographer of the Year (1975), director of photography at *The Oklahoman*, freelance magazine writer for *Sports Illustrated, Sports Illustrated for Kids, Entrepreneur, Business Week, Progressive Grocer, Working Woman, Newsweek,* and *Texaco.*

Chris Lee (1955-), worked with KBFL Radio and with the University of Missouri NBC affiliate KOMU-TV, news photographer and chief photographer for KOCO in Oklahoma City, helped to design the First Alert Storm Team, covered the Star School explosion, the May 3, 1999 tornado outbreak, Hurricane Katrina, and the Oklahoma City bombing.

Ray Lokey (1953-2017), third-generation newspaper publisher at the *Johnston County Capital-Democrat*, news editor for the Southeastern Oklahoma State University paper, public information officer at Murray State College, named Johnston County Chamber of Commerce's 2002 Citizen of the Year, Oklahoma Press Association president (2003), recipient of the Milt Phillips Award.

Kim Poindexter (1960-), worked with the *Cherokee County Chronicle* and the *Tahlequah Daily Press*, which has won three national social media awards and several Oklahoma Press Association Sequoyah sweepstakes awards, recipient of more than 40 first-place editorial and column writing awards, mentor to many young journalists.

George Tomek (1939-), worked with KOTV, WKY-TV, KOCO-TV, OETA, KMOX-TV, and KDFW-TV, news director at KTVY/KFOR, recipient of a national IRIS Award for the investigative miniseries "The Gospel According to TV," recipient of several James Scripps Awards, served as a captain in the U.S. Navy Reserve.

Berry Tramel (1961-), beat writer, assistant sports editor, sports editor, and columnist for *The Oklahoman*, worked with the *Norman Transcript*, six-time winner of Oklahoma's Sportswriter of the Year, recipient of five Dallas Press Club Katie Awards, part of a staff that won The Associated Press Sports Grand Slam award four times in six years.

— **2019**

M.J. Alexander (1961-), photographer, reporter, and editor with newspapers, magazines, and The Associated Press, author and illustrator of two fine-art books, one of which won an Oklahoma Book Award, first Oklahoman featured in a solo exhibition in the Main Gallery of the International Photography Hall of Fame.

Mary Bishop-Baldwin (1961-), assistant editor and copy editor at the *Tulsa World*, journalism professor at East Central University, worked with the *Bristow News & Record Citizen* and *The Daily Oklahoman*, recipient of a Newsmakers Award from the Association for Women in Communications, named a 2014 Oklahoman of the Year.

Brian Blansett (1952-), recipient of the Oklahoma Press Association sweepstakes award, city editor at the *Waco Tribune-Herald*, owner of the *Tri-County Herald* newspaper in Meeker, professor at Baylor University and Oklahoma Baptist University, elected to the North Rock Creek board of education, Oklahoma Press Association president (2017), veteran of the U.S. Air Force and the 45th Infantry.

Ziva Branstetter (1964-), worked with the *Guthrie Daily Leader, Tulsa Tribune,* and *Philadelphia Daily News,* investigative reporter, city editor, and enterprise editor at the *Tulsa World,* senior editor at The Center for Investigative Reporting, hired by *The Washington Post* to lead a new reporting team focused on corporate accountability.

Chris Casteel (1959-), worked with *The Daily Oklahoman* and the *Oklahoma City Times,* documented major political events for more than 25 years in Washington, named news director for *The Oklahoman* (2018), Washington Gridiron Club member and past membership chairman of the National Press Club.

Bob Dotson (1946-), worked with WKY-TV, recipient of Oklahoma's first national Emmy, NBC News correspondent, winner of seven and nominee of 11 national Emmys, ran his series "The American Story with Bob Dotson" on the *Today Show* for 40 years, producer of *El Capitan's Courageous Climbers,* which won seven International Film Festivals and the CINE Grand Prize; grand prize recipient of the DuPont Columbia, Robert F. Kennedy, and William Allen White awards, recipient of a record six Edward R. Murrow Awards for Best Network News Writing.

Wayne Greene (1963-), city editor, then editorial pages editor at the *Tulsa World,* worked with the *Enid Morning News and Enid News Eagle,* recipient of the University of Oklahoma Distinguished Alumni Award (2017), named "The Conscience of the Community" by the Tulsa Regional Chamber of Commerce (2016).

Griff Palmer (1956-), worked for the *Bartlesville Examiner-Enterprise* and *Stillwater News Press,* assistant city editor at the *Oklahoma City Times* and *The Daily Oklahoman,* first database editor for *The Oklahoman,* database editor at *The San Jose Mercury News,* worked with *The New York Times,* where he contributed to two Pulitzer-winning projects.

Timothy E. Talley (1952-), worked with The Associated Press for nearly 25 years, and with the *Plaquemine Post* and the *Morning Advocate* and *State-Times,* two-time recipient of the Louisiana Bar Association's top journalism prize, helped cover the criminal trials of the Oklahoma City bombing conspirators.

2020

the changes for a special anniversary

The rules for the Oklahoma Journalism Hall of Fame were like gold laid in concrete.

Nine Hall of Famers had been selected every year since its inception. All were honored at a luncheon or afternoon reception at the University of Central Oklahoma.

That all changed for the golden anniversary.

Instead of the usual number in the previous 49 classes, the 10-member Selection Committee chose 10 new Hall of Fame members for 2020. Over a two-year period, it also chose 10 for the second posthumous class. The first posthumous class in 2005 for the 35th anniversary inducted eight members.

Thus, 20 journalists will be inducted into the Hall of Fame in 2020. They are pioneers and leaders in radio, newspapers, and television, multiple national award winners or national office holders, war correspondents and heroes, legendary sportswriters, columnists, and editors who stood up for civil rights and the least of us, and the ultimate father. Some were born in the 1800s and ended their careers in the 1960s.

Others were born in the 1960s and continue their stellar careers today.

Two Lifetime Achievement Award honorees were also selected, both with special connections already to the Hall of Fame and a lifetime of service to either Oklahoma or the nation. That made a total of six for the Hall of Fame's 50 years.

The ceremony time was changed to an evening ceremony on April 24, 2020. And the site was changed for the first time ever from the University of Central Oklahoma to the Oklahoma History Center.

The ceremony will return to the University of Central Oklahoma for the 51st class. Many of the rules will return.

But the 2020 classes have stood out for many reasons, far beyond how their inductions changed golden traditions for the 50th anniversary.

Lori Fullbright on a 2019 trip to Amman, Jordan to cover a story about the Tulsa Police, the only U.S. Team to compete in the international Warrior Games.

Lori Fullbright and photographer Oscar Pea on a 1998 trip to London to do ride-alongs with Bobbies (police officers), observing differences from law enforcement in Oklahoma.

Gloria Brown and third-generation publisher Rusty Ferguson in front of the *Perry Daily Journal*.

Lori Fullbright on a 1995 trip to the Adriatic Sea, covering the Oklahoma Marines who rescued Captain Scott O'Grady when he was shot down over Bosnia.

Tony Stizza (left) films an interview with Oklahoma City National Memorial & Museum executive director Kari Watkins as she talks about the wreaths being placed on the chairs at the Memorial. Photo by Lauren Long. December 2, 2019.

The Oklahoman reporter Michael McNutt and *Tulsa World* reporter Barbara Hoberock take advantage of the opportunity to question Oklahoma Governor Mary Fallin after her appearance at the Oklahoma Press Association Convention on Friday, June 8, 2012, in Midwest City, Oklahoma. Photo by Steve Sisney, *The Oklahoman*. Courtesy of the *Tulsa World*.

SCOTT THOMPSON
the ultimate father's choice about journalism's ultimate honor
By Joe Hight, 2013 Inductee

Scott Thompson had to make a choice in early 2019—attend his son's concert at Princeton University or his induction into the Oklahoma Journalism Hall of Fame.

I had called to inform him that he had been chosen by the 10-member Selection Committee for induction with the 49th class. However, all inductees are required to attend the induction ceremony or face having their nominations resubmitted for consideration the next year.

For most of his career in Tulsa television, as many in his field do, the five-time national Edward R. Murrow Award winner had to work evenings. When his son, Will, was born in 1995, he was a weekend anchor who worked three evenings a week as a reporter. By the time Jack was born in 1999, Thompson was a nightly anchor.

The schedule gave him time to spend days with his children. But in the evenings, "I never had dinner with them," Thompson said in that distinctive voice of a news anchor. "That really got to me."

He did say he would rush home to read books to his sons during the evenings, but then had to "dash back to read the news" on air.

So, when the first call about his induction came, Thompson's choice was easy. "I didn't want to miss any more of my children's events," he said. "I had done that my entire career."

While other members were being inducted into the 2019 Hall of Fame, Thompson was on his way to New Jersey to hear Jack play the bassoon in the Princeton Symphony Orchestra. An audition the year before had helped garner Jack's acceptance into the Ivy League Princeton, one of the 1,100 admitted out of 47,000 applications. His oldest son, Will, is in the doctoral program at the University of Delaware.

"The concert was beautiful," said Thompson, who admitted his sons may be smarter because he read books to them and they never watched

Scott Thompson with son Jack; wife, Holly; and son, Will.

his nightly newscasts because of the content.

Several months later, I made a second call to Thompson to inform him that he had been chosen for the 50th class. I had told him in the first call that I respected his decision and hinted that, while not guaranteed, he probably would be selected the next year.

This time, there were no fatherly conflicts on April 24, 2020, three days after his 59th birthday. He could attend.

Scott Thompson and the KOTV News on 6 crew during his final newscast in 2017.

Scott Thompson with his sons, Will and Jack.

WILLIAM RUSSELL MOORE
the journalist who became a war hero
By Joe Hight, 2013 Inductee

William Russell Moore was a war correspondent who became a war hero.

Although the Oklahoma native is listed in some historical texts, he was unknown to most in his home state until Paul Roales sent an email to the Oklahoma Journalism Hall of Fame. Roales said he was a military historian who had researched Moore, born March 25, 1910 in Nowata.

"I think he should be in the Oklahoma Journalism Hall of Fame," Roales wrote.

Moore's name will join the Hall of Fame in 2020 as part of the second posthumous class inducted in the Hall of Fame's 50-year history.

Here's an edited excerpt of the story that Roales tells about Moore:

After receiving a bachelor's degree from the University of Oklahoma in 1932, Moore worked for *The Daily Oklahoman* until 1937 when he was first hired by The Associated Press in Denver.

Five years later in September 1942, he was commissioned a second lieutenant upon his graduation from the Anti-aircraft Artillery Officer Candidate School at Camp Davis. He served in the Army forces in the Pacific during World War II from 1942-1946 and was discharged with the rank of major after serving in Korea. He rejoined The Associated Press in New York, and in April 1948 was sent to Korea as a staff correspondent.

Moore's dispatches told graphically of the growing tension between [the] north and south. When the North Korean invasion finally broke on June 25, he was in Hong Kong on vacation. Immediately he volunteered to fly back to Korea. He was one of the first reporters to reach the front lines and was first to report the atrocity of captured Americans who had been shot with their hands tied behind their backs. He died on July 31, 1950, while helping U.S. soldiers hit by North Korean gunfire.

His body was found five years later.

Roales also found a story dated October 30, 1950, in the *Greeley (Colorado) Daily Tribune* that included an officer's description of the man he met over a cup of coffee.

"Nice fellow. Real friendly and a real storyteller," Captain Carl M. Anderson said. "When the shells were falling around us I heard him praying ou[t] loud."

The paper also reported that "Moore's cool, level-headed quality of thinking ahead … made his dispatches stand out."

Moore, who was unmarried when he died at 40, is enshrined with the nearly 2,350 journalists killed worldwide in the Newseum's Journalists Memorial.

Because of Roales, he now will be forever remembered in the Oklahoma Journalism Hall of Fame.

BLACKBURN, GOODWIN, BETZ, WEBB, FOOTE, & RIDENOUR
the Lifetime Achievers
By Emily Siddiqui, Student Editor

Journalistic endeavors would not be effective without the support and leadership of fellow truth-seeking, world-changing individuals within the community.

The Oklahoma Journalism Hall of Fame has extended its reach of recognition by deciding to grant up to two Lifetime Achievement Awards each year. The award honors outstanding individuals whom the Selection Committee deems worthy, even though they may not have been journalists themselves or spent their entire careers in journalism.

"The Lifetime Achievement Award is given to individuals who have steadfastly emulated the values and principles of journalists through their work in the community or through leading initiatives that train or support journalists, future generations of journalists, or the Hall of Fame

itself," said Joe Hight, Oklahoma Journalism Hall of Fame Director.

The first Lifetime Achievement Award was given in 1992 as a "Certificate of Merit" to Windsor Ridenour for his leadership and 28 years of service to journalism just before the *Tulsa Tribune* closed in September 1992. The Hall of Fame's Executive Committee decided in 2019 to credit Ridenour with a Lifetime Achievement Award.

The Lifetime Achievement Award was officially initiated in 2018 with the naming of Dr. Joe Foote as the recipient.

Here are the recipients starting with 2020's two honorees:

— 2020

Dr. Bob Blackburn (1951-) has a passion for history and government that comes alive through his own life's work. As executive director of the Oklahoma Historical Society since 1999, he helped to plan and build the Oklahoma History Center museum, now home to more than 50 educational topics and 2,000 artifacts. His involvement with the OHS began in 1980, serving as editor of *The Chronicles of Oklahoma*. He has co-written nearly 20 books as well as numerous articles, journal entries, and screenplays. He is known for his historical knowledge of Oklahoma journalism and his many friendships with journalists. Journalism also is part of his heritage. His mother, Ida B. Blackburn, known as "Ida B," was inducted into the Oklahoma Journalism Hall of Fame in 2001.

Robert K. "Bob" Goodwin (1948-) shares a long family history of service in journalism, community leadership, and civil rights. As the fourth of his family to receive recognition from the Oklahoma Journalism Hall of Fame, Goodwin continues that legacy. He stopped short of earning a doctorate to take over his family's newspaper,

The Oklahoma Eagle, where he became an award-winning columnist and helped the newspaper staff receive state and national awards. President George H.W. Bush later named Goodwin the executive director of the White House Initiative on Historically Black Colleges and Universities, a role Goodwin filled for two years. He later joined Points of Light, an international nonprofit, non-partisan organization dedicated to solving serious social problems through encouraging voluntary service. In his 15 years there, 12 as CEO, he was instrumental in several successful initiatives, including the President's Summit for America's Future. Goodwin has received numerous awards for his work, including four honorary doctorate degrees. He was named one of the 50 most influential leaders in the nonprofit sector by *The NonProfit Times* nine years in a row.

— 2019

Dr. Don Betz served in administration and as President at Northeastern State University from 1971-1994; Provost/Vice President for Academic Affairs at Palmer College of Chiropractic in Davenport, Iowa; consultant for the United Nations (1982-2003); Provost/Vice President for Academic Affairs and President for the University of Central Oklahoma; and Chancellor of the University of Wisconsin-River Falls. He is known for his steadfast support of journalism, including student journalism, First Amendment freedoms and the Oklahoma Journalism Hall of Fame.

Dr. W. Roger Webb served 12 years with the Oklahoma Department of Public Safety, Commissioner of Public Safety for the State of Oklahoma (1974-78), served on the Board of Directors for the International Association of Chiefs of Police, and as President of Northeastern State University and the University of Central Oklahoma. Webb was honored for his commitment to the Oklahoma Journalism Hall of Fame and in giving it permanent status in the Nigh University Center at the University of Central Oklahoma.

— 2018

Dr. Joe Foote was a journalist for multiple radio stations, an author, founder of the World Journalism Education Council, Dean of the Gaylord College at the University of Oklahoma (now Dean Emeritus), Director of the Walter Cronkite School at Arizona State, journalism dean at Southern Illinois University, professor at Cornell, press secretary for Speaker Carl Albert, and chief of staff for Congressman Dave McCurdy. He was honored for his lifetime achievement of mentoring and fostering excellence in journalism education.

— 1992

Windsor Ridenour was a journalist and leader who started as a reporter for the *Tulsa Tribune*. He became the Oklahoma City bureau chief, then city editor and assistant managing editor before becoming executive editor in 1989. He held the position for three years until the *Tribune* closed in 1992 as one of the last metro afternoon papers. He directed award-winning projects from a series on the riots at the Oklahoma State Penitentiary that won the 1983 Associated Press Sweepstakes Award to stories about the Penn Square Bank collapse. He was a past president of the AP-Oklahoma News Executives and Tulsa Press Club. His award's original name "Certificate of Merit" in 1992 was changed to "Lifetime Achievement" in 2019. He was the second to receive the certificate.

TIM CHAVEZ

short stories about a Hall of Famer who inspired others

By Kathi Cox McClure

The marker on Tim Chavez's grave says, "For the least of these."

Chavez always sought to include those who were ignored. He spoke up for the least of these all through his journalism career, no matter the politics of the particular paper he worked for. From inserting subtle liberal tidbits in his TV column for *The Sunday Oklahoman*, which had a conservative editorial page, to initiating citywide racial discussions for the *Observer-Dispatch* in Utica, New York, and including conservative voices in his groundbreaking "Equal Time" column in the liberal-leaning *Tennessean*, he was a voice for many.

His gift, and his goal, was inspiring the passion in others that he felt in his very soul.

Chavez also had a knack for marketing.

In March of his first year as opinion page editor in Utica, New York, he wrote a column bemoaning the winter's lack of snow—"I have more snow in my freezer than we've had here."

The next Saturday the blizzard of 1993 dumped 35.6 inches on Utica. In penance, Chavez wore a shirt and shorts and perched for hours atop a massive pile of snow. He sat in a lawn chair and read the newspaper in freezing temperatures.

Utica residents—a hard-to-please group—loved it. And Chavez, and the newspaper, won a lot of goodwill that day.

And Chavez had a canine-like ability to sniff out news. He found stories everywhere. Driving to the store one day, he spied a man walking on the side of a middle Tennessee road with a man-sized cross on his shoulder.

Chavez pulled over, whipped out the reporter's notebook he always had in his back pocket, and ran after the man to get his story. The man, depending on the charity of passersby, was walking across the country to proclaim God's love.

Tim's work always personified what it took to serve the least of these.

Kathi Cox McClure, a longtime journalist, was Tim Chavez's wife when he died of leukemia in 2009. His last blog post on May 10, 2009 led with these words: "Every person has a book in them, but first you must have an ending that enlightens and inspires." In the blog, he added, " ... My story is not over yet."

Tim Chavez, dressed in a shirt and shorts, sits atop a pile of snow in Utica, New York after the blizzard of 1993.

A.J. SMITHERMAN

the influence and contributions of "Big Daddy"

By Raven Majia Williams

In contemplating an appropriate title for the biography I wrote about my great-grandfather, a man my family refers to as "Big Daddy," it became evident that out of the many contributions he made to the black and Native American races, as well as to Oklahoma's white citizens who benefited from his peacemaking, three in particular have had the most significant impact on

American history. Hence the title:

A.J. Smitherman: Black Gold, Black Wall Street & Black Power.

The first of Smitherman's major contributions was his work to help Native Americans and Freedmen (blacks born on reservations) retain possession of their "Black Gold." Black Gold was a term for the oil that was discovered in Oklahoma on land allotted to Native Americans and Freedmen by the U.S. government. Native Americans and Freedmen were supposed to be given 160 acres of land for every man, woman, and child. In many cases that land struck oil. The amount of wealth that Native Americans and Freedmen retained as a result of Smitherman's help is not quantifiable, but is estimated to be in the hundreds of millions of dollars.

The second contribution is Smitherman's influence in shaping not only what blacks were thinking and doing in the thriving Greenwood District in Tulsa, also known as Black Wall Street, but throughout the nation: His newspaper, the **Tulsa Star**, was distributed throughout the United States. And as President of the Western Negro Press Association for 11 consecutive years, he influenced other editors who were helping to shape their communities as well.

A political visionary and activist, Smitherman may have made his most important contribution what he called his "great experiment" of persuading blacks to diversify their vote rather than vote straight Republican as they had since Abraham Lincoln freed the slaves. He saw that Republicans were doing nothing to earn the black vote that they took for granted, and Democrats were doing nothing to earn the black vote because they believed they'd never get it. In a letter he wrote to Governor James B.A. Robertson in March 1922, after his exile to Boston, he described the mission's success:

"Prior to June 1, 1921, I was editor and publisher of the *Tulsa Star*, the only colored Democratic newspaper in the country, and it was through the influence of my paper that the political complexion of the colored people of Tulsa was decidedly changed from Republican to Democratic majorities. Not only that, throughout the state colored people were influenced to diversify their politics and to support their friends in the Democratic party as well as the Republican party, as in no other southern state, and the Star blazed the way."

And still today the majority of blacks in America vote Democrat.

Growing up, my father would share stories of "Big Daddy." He would regularly recite the epic poem "Big Daddy" wrote about the Tulsa Race Massacre of 1921. My father could rarely get through the poem's entirety without pausing with emotion. One particular story my father shared was about the time "Big Daddy" confronted a lynch mob about to hang a black man. Armed with only a briefcase filled with newspapers, "Big Daddy" yelled, "This briefcase is filled with four bottles of Nitroglycerin. If you don't release that man immediately, I'm gonna throw it, and we will all burn in hell!" Stunned, the mob turned and ran, their victim saved from certain hanging.

So, it is no surprise that the many scholars and historians who have written about our "Big Daddy" have all in one way or another been moved to do so by what is an undeniable respect for the man's courage, drive, and commitment to uplift and protect his race.

The fact that he has received little historical recognition is something that I am determined to change. It's unfortunate that his legacy has not been celebrated more after making a conscious decision to lose everything to empower his race. His humility played a large part in this, as he raised his children and they raised theirs to not value things like fame. One of my favorite quotes from "Big Daddy" is:

"There is just enough difference between celebrity and notoriety to make one hesitate before aspiring to the possession of either."

Well, I'm sorry "Big Daddy." I'm committed to seeing you get the rightful credit you deserve as one of the most courageous and influential journalists in American history.

B.A. BRIDGEWATER
the value of a $2 bill
By John D. Ferguson

Growing up in the 1950s, my father, John A. Ferguson, would bring home from work around Christmas time an envelope with a card inside addressed to me.

The card was from B.A. Bridgewater, who was my dad's boss as the sports editor of the *Tulsa World*. Inside the card was a crisp, brand new $2 bill.

My dad would always force me at ages 7-, 8- and 9-years-old to call Mr. Bridgewater and thank him for the gift. I was reluctant, but did it anyway.

After my ninth birthday, Mr. Bridgewater approved my dad bringing me to the *Tulsa World* on the Friday after Thanksgiving. It was like "Bring your son to work day."

After getting an early tour of the office and back shop where the paper was put together, I got pretty bored. Little did I know that my boredom would soon be broken.

I was told to answer the phone and give out basketball or football scores as requested. Scores came fresh off the AP machine in the soundproof room next door. When you walked inside you heard the cacophony of the typing terminals spewing out reams of rolled paper.

I learned quickly that the scores of the game were less important than the point spread. I went from saying "Notre Dame 27, Maryland 20" to "Notre Dame by seven."
The hours flew quickly with my new assignment, all thanks to Mr. Bridgewater and my dad.

And, yes, I got paid for these eight hours of work. I received yet another $2 bill.

B.A. Bridgewater hired John A. Ferguson as a Tulsa World *Sportswriter. Both are being inducted posthumously into the 2020 Oklahoma Journalism Hall of Fame.*

THE 50TH ANNIVERSARY CLASS

Clytie Bunyan (1961-) has seen the business scene change drastically in her 30-plus years in Oklahoma. She started as an entry-level reporter and is now coordinator of the internship program and staff development at *The Oklahoman*. She was the first woman and the longest-serving business editor, and in 2012 was named director of Business & Lifestyles. Her responsibilities expanded to being editor of the health, common education, and city hall beats.

Al Eschbach (1945-) is considered by some as the father of sports talk radio. One listener in 1976 didn't think a Jersey City guy would make it as a sports announcer in Oklahoma, but four decades later, his broadcasts are more popular than ever. He worked for the *Oklahoma Daily* at OU, *Norman Transcript*, and *The Oklahoma Journal*. He started at KTOK as sports director in 1976 and has worked for various radio and TV stations since. Eschbach is in the Oklahoma Broadcasters Hall of Fame and teaches at the University of Oklahoma's Gaylord College.

Rusty Ferguson (1961-) comes from a family dedicated to newspapers and their communities. The 3rd-generation publisher of the *Cleveland American, The Hominy News-Progress*, and *The Pawnee Chief* was president of the Oklahoma Press Association in 2012 and served as the Cleveland Chamber of Commerce president three times. He is the fourth member of the Ferguson family to be inducted into the Oklahoma Journalism Hall of Fame— his grandfather Jo. O., his uncle D. Jo, and his father, Larry.

Lori Fullbright (1966-) knew at age 12 she would be a TV reporter. The Bolivar, Missouri native followed her dream, starting at Missouri stations before moving to KOTV in Tulsa, where for 27 years, she has specialized in crime reporting. She has dedicated her career to sharing victim stories with sensitivity and telling stories that are fact-based and balanced. Civic work in crime prevention and promoting key women's issues has earned her many awards. She has reported nationally and internationally on Oklahomans, including on the American military in Iraq, Bosnia, and at sea.

Rochelle Hines (1963-) covered major Oklahoma tragedies during her media career in the 22 years she worked for The Associated Press. Her work included covering the Oklahoma City bombing, the 1999 tornado, and the execution of several inmates at the Oklahoma State Penitentiary. Her stories at the University of Oklahoma's *Oklahoma Daily* about two teenagers on Oklahoma's death row earned her the Hearst Award.

Michael McNutt (1952-) has covered all types of stories during his more than 30 years at *The Oklahoman*. Oklahoma's governors and lawmakers as well as state agency leaders knew the dedicated reporter who routinely worked 15- to 16-hour days on the capitol beat. He was named to the *Washington Post's* list of best state-based political reporters in 2013. And he knows all about rural Oklahoma, venturing to places few residents have heard of. McNutt worked for Governor Mary Fallin, first as her press secretary and then as communications director. He later became communications director for the juvenile affairs office.

Michael Sims (1954-) began his TV broadcasting career at KWTV, eventually becoming managing editor. Also, early in his career, he was a reporter and anchor for both the KOMA and WKY radio news stations. Skills gained in Oklahoma took him to the national market, where he helped the industry transition to the digital newsroom. He guided CBS through the change to digital that now includes news coverage for every conceivable platform. Later he joined ABC News as executive director and general manager of the Network News Service, a landmark video cooperative owned and operated by ABC News, CBS News, and FOX News.

Tony Stizza (1957-) worked more than 26 years at KTVY, now KFOR in Oklahoma City, filming documentaries such as "Tapestry" and "Strangers in Their Own Land." His dedication has earned 16 Emmy Awards, three National Press Photographer's Association regional photographer of the year awards, and numerous other awards. He is now video director for the Oklahoma City National Memorial & Museum. He is a member of the Oklahoma Association of Broadcasters Hall of Fame.

Scott Thompson (1961-), longtime main news anchor at KOTV in Tulsa, is also widely known as the station's "Oklahoma Traveler" for the long-running series that took him to every continent except Antarctica. He began his career at his hometown Illinois newspaper and worked at KRCG-TV in Jefferson City, Missouri. Moving to Tulsa in 1987, he worked at KJRH-TV before joining KOTV. He earned six national Edward R. Murrow Awards, eight regional Emmy Awards and the national Sigma Delta

Chi Bronze Medallion for Public Service in Television Journalism. His best reward comes from time spent with his wife, Holly, and two sons, Will and Jack.

Yvette Walker (1961-), former news director at *The Oklahoman*, is assistant dean for student affairs at the University of Oklahoma's Gaylord College. She has served on the Society of Professional Journalists national board and the FOI Oklahoma advisory board and is a member of the National Association of Black Journalists. She was the Edith Kinney Gaylord Journalism Ethics Chair at the University of Central Oklahoma. She has worked for medium to large news media in Indiana, Michigan, Missouri, and Texas.

THE 50TH ANNIVERSARY POSTHUMOUS CLASS

B.A. Bridgewater (1894-1964) may be the only person in the newspaper industry who, as a managing editor, hired himself to be a sports editor. "Bridge" held the *Tulsa World* position for 37 years and wrote a "Telling the World" column. In 1959, Oklahoma State University bestowed its only "Oklahoma Sports Writer" award to the "grand old man" of sports. In 1960, according to his obituary, OSU discontinued the award because "no one could follow Bridge."

Tim Chavez (1958-2009) worked for *The Oklahoman* before becoming an opinion page editor for the *Observer-Dispatch* in Utica, New York. He then became a reporter and political columnist for *The Tennessean*. He won three national awards from the Education Writers Association and the Will Rogers Humanitarian Award from the National Society of Newspaper Columnists.

Charles Cagle (1937-2015) began his career throwing newspapers, then worked in several departments at the *Harrison Daily Times* (Arkansas) and was managing editor at the *Clinton Daily News*. In 1975, he joined Neighbor Newspapers (later CNHI) in suburban Tulsa as general manager for 19 newspapers. His 61 years in the news business included being named a Half Century Club member by the Oklahoma Press Association.

John A. Ferguson, Jr. (1925-2000) had a passion for writing about sports stars for nearly 50 years. Young athletes and internationally known athletes were part of his beat. "Fergy" wrote "The Bullpen" column for the *Tulsa World*. He was a leader, bringing young *World* staff writers along as they started their careers.

Don Gammill (1952-2017) had a varied career that extended beyond the four walls of a newspaper office. He held the traditional roles as a sportswriter and other various editorial positions, including editor and columnist, during his career at the *Enid News & Eagle* and *The Oklahoman*. He taught young journalists and reached out to the community to teach high school students, co-founding the Newsroom 101 program at *The Oklahoman*.

Helen Holmes (1915-1997) wrote for newspapers, taught journalism, and was honored for her historical writing about Guthrie's early days, work that was recognized by state leaders after her death. The former Guthrie mayor is a member of the U.S. Army Women's Foundation and the Oklahoma Historians and Oklahoma Women's halls of fame.

William E. Lehmann (1928-2016) As publisher of the *Guthrie Daily Leader*, he galvanized support to save the state's first capital building and other historic sites in that city. His column "By the Way" was named the National Newspaper Association's Best Humorous Column of the Year in 1973.

Marjorie Paxson (1923-2017) was one of the first woman publishers in the country. She spent 42 years in the newspaper industry, serving as a writer and holding various editorial positions for United Press, Associated Press, *Houston Post, Houston Chronicle, Miami Herald,* and *St. Petersburg Times.* She continued to write columns for the *Muskogee Phoenix* after her retirement as publisher in 1986. She also served as national president for Women in Communications.

A.J. Smitherman (1883-1961) was an African-American press pioneer and political activist. In 1913, he founded the *Tulsa Star*, America's first black Democratic nationally distributed newspaper. Smitherman highlighted the achievements and challenges of blacks throughout the country and encouraged them to use their constitutional rights to vote, and to defend themselves against mob rule and lynchings. During the Tulsa Race Massacre of 1921, Smitherman's newspaper and home were destroyed, and he and his family were forced to flee. Eventually Smitherman settled in Buffalo, New York, where he launched the *Buffalo Star*. Smitherman continued to advocate for his race and provide leadership to his community until his death in 1961.

William Russell Moore (1910-1950) probably never heard of Korea as a boy in Nowata, Oklahoma. But, after starting at *The Oklahoman*, he would join The Associated Press and distinguish himself as a war correspondent who gave his life helping wounded American soldiers. He was one of 90 correspondents killed during the Korean War. He served in the Army for four years during World War II and was promoted to the rank of major before being discharged.

EPILOGUE
the changing traditions of the Hall of Fame

By Joe Hight, 2013 Inductee

That phone call is a tradition.

When you receive one telling you that you've been selected for induction into the Oklahoma Journalism Hall of Fame, it changes your life. It tells you that you've reached the pinnacle of your career.

When I received that call, I was stunned. I can't say it wasn't a goal, especially after nominating several Hall of Fame members. But I thought the call was a distant possibility, especially after I had moved to Colorado.

But Terry Clark changed my life when he made the call to me in early 2013. And I am forever grateful to Mike Shannon, a Hall of Fame member who wrote my letter of nomination.

For the last three years, I've been making that call. I have received responses such as, "I never thought this would happen." And, "This is by far my biggest honor." Some new members have broken into tears upon hearing the news. Several asked me to repeat what I had just told them.

I always ask one question to make sure they understand, "Do you accept induction into the Oklahoma Journalism Hall of Fame?"

The best response came from Clytie Bunyan in 2019: "Are you crazy? Are you kidding me? Why wouldn't I? Of course, I will accept induction!"

That's why that one-on-one call will never change as a Hall of Fame tradition. But other traditions may change.

The Oklahoma Journalism Hall of Fame was built on tradition. Hall of Fame inductees were usually chosen from major publications and broadcast outlets in Oklahoma, were leaders of community news organizations, or they had won major awards while working at out-of-state institutions while still having long-standing connections to Oklahoma.

The Selection Committee has followed in that tradition, with traditional outlets receiving more nominations and thus more selections.

However, the disruption in the media is changing all that. It will change the Hall of Fame, too.

New members may still come from those long-standing news organizations with historic roots in Oklahoma. They will still have to be nominated, have at least 10 years of experience, strong connections to the state and accomplishments that extend beyond their news organizations.

Future selections, however, won't be confined to the traditional outlets or jobs. They could come from areas such as database, sports, online journalism, podcasts, blogs, and social media.

But the one criterion that will remain consistent is a question that Vance Harrison, president of the Oklahoma Association of Broadcasters, asked during the 2019 selection process:

"Are they journalists?" Defined as those individuals who collect, write, distribute, or broadcast news and information to the public; who stand up for the First Amendment, especially for freedom of the press, and freedom of information, and those who hold truth and ethics as their standards.

They who proudly declare "I am a journalist" before anything else in their life's work.

Those are the ones who will receive the Hall of Fame calls of the future, no matter where they work in the media.

ACKNOWLEDGMENTS

By Joe Hight, 2013 Inductee

A book filled with personal essays, stories, and photos and called *Our Greatest Journalists: The 50th Anniversary of the Oklahoma Journalism Hall of Fame* could be considered a lofty goal.

I wondered whether such a book was possible even as I created an outline of topics and essays. Several people told me that I shouldn't pursue such a project because it took too much time, work, or money.

However, from the onset, a small group of individuals dedicated themselves to working with me to solicit essays, writing them, scouring for photos that could be used and editing the many words used in this book. Most of them volunteered to do it, too.

So, in acknowledging those contributions, it's important that the names Ralph Schaefer, Lindel Hutson, Billie Rodely, and Emily Siddiqui receive the utmost praise for what they accomplished. Ralph and Lindel served as the first editors of the essays while also providing other content for the book. Ralph worked countless hours with Emily in creating the short biographies and photos for every Hall of Fame member. Billie provided and solicited content while also planning the script and production of the short documentary with Hall of Fame member Bill Perry. Jennifer Gilliland is another contributor who constantly provided us with space for our planning meetings at the Oklahoma Press Association while also providing insight, and editing and soliciting content.

Ralph, Lindel, Billie, and Jennifer are on the Hall of Fame's Executive Committee with me, and this book would not have been possible without their support and hard work. Ralph especially became an enthusiastic and constant contributor in working with Emily on completing this massive project, confirming names and facts, and working with me on other aspects of the Oklahoma Journalism Hall of Fame's 50th anniversary.

Emily was a University of Central Oklahoma junior when I hired her for this project. She probably had no idea that she would become the organizer of content, a writer of essays and stories, and a videographer for the essay on Vance Trimble. She also has the best copy-editing eyes that I've seen for a person of her age. I will add her to the list of some of the best hires I've ever made because she was that instrumental in this book's creation.

Many Oklahoma Journalism Hall of Fame members, such as past longtime director Terry Clark, and a few who are not in the Hall of Fame were involved in the creation of this special book commemorating the 50-year anniversary. When asked, they didn't hesitate to step up to provide essays about other Hall of Fame members or to provide personal experiences to enhance the book.

Others deserve our thanks as well: Dr. Bob Blackburn and the Oklahoma History Center provided numerous photos. John Greiner not only provided essays, but photos from his many years at the State Capitol. Ed Kelley volunteered essays beyond what he was asked to write. Don Sherry and Steve Lackmeyer were among those not in the Hall of Fame who wrote essays. Friend Terri Folks provided a photo of *The Vista* newsroom that was used in the book. Karisa Rollins of the UCO Foundation became vital in helping me solicit donated funds for the book, documentary, and other improvements to the Hall of Fame. Lisa Kern is the Hall of Fame's financial adviser, the person who works behind the scenes with me and a vital individual for the Hall's annual success. Lauren Bieri of UCO Photographic Services provided portrait photos. Mary Carver, Mark Zimmerman, Bradley Kiem, Teddy Burch, Amber Loomis, Rachael Wood, and Patty Gass, from the UCO Mass Communication Department, are invaluable in their work and support of the Hall of Fame. And, finally, Gini Moore Campbell of the Oklahoma Hall of Fame was enthusiastic about the concept from the start and provided insight, support, and her editing skills to publish the book.

But the most important creators of *Our Greatest Journalists* are those who lived the lives that are portrayed in this book. I and others involved in this book's creation came to know them personally as we pored over their biographies and photos. I grew to admire many of them more than I had already.

I wish we could have written an essay on all of them, but that wasn't possible. However, their legacies will live on because of a Hall of Fame conceived simply by Dr. Ray Tassin and Dennie Hall.

Those two in the end are whom each Hall of Fame member who receives Oklahoma's greatest journalistic honor should thank the most.

The book's editing team, from left to right: Joe Hight, Billie Rodely, Emily Siddiqui, Lindel Hutson, and Ralph Schaefer. 2019, UCO Photographic Services.

Members of the Oklahoma Journalism Hall of Fame Executive Committee, from left to right: Billie Rodely, Joe Hight, Jennifer Gilliland, Ralph Schaefer, and Lindel Hutson. 2019, UCO Photographic Services.

INDEX